THE SPANISH CONQUERORS

ABRAHAM LINCOLN EDITION

∴

VOLUME 2
THE CHRONICLES
OF AMERICA SERIES
ALLEN JOHNSON
EDITOR

GERHARD R. LOMER
CHARLES W. JEFFERYS
ASSISTANT EDITORS

CHRISTOPHORVS COLVMBVS

Gravure, Andersen-Lamb. Co. N.Y.

THE
SPANISH CONQUERORS

A CHRONICLE OF THE
DAWN OF EMPIRE OVERSEAS
BY IRVING BERDINE RICHMAN

NEW HAVEN: YALE UNIVERSITY PRESS
TORONTO: GLASGOW, BROOK & CO.
LONDON: HUMPHREY MILFORD
OXFORD UNIVERSITY PRESS
1919

ILLUSTRATIONS

CHRISTOPHER COLUMBUS

Painting in the Marine Museum, Madrid, reproduced in Avery's *History of the United States*.

No portrait of Columbus is known to have been painted from life or during his lifetime. Of the supposed portraits now existing, the earliest is a wood engraving in *Elogia Virorum Illustrium*, by Paulus Jovius, published in 1575. This is said to have been copied from a painting in a collection of portraits at the Villa of Jovius on Lake Como. The collection has been dispersed, and the Columbus portrait (if it ever existed) has disappeared. This woodcut doubtless was the model for an engraving by Aliprando Capriolo, published in Rome in 1596. On these two engravings have been based the greater number of the many imaginary portraits of Columbus.

Two other portraits of considerable antiquity are known. The Florence Gallery contains a painting attributed to Cristofano dell' Altissimo, said to be of a date earlier than 1568. A copy of this portrait was made for Thomas Jefferson in 1784, and is now in the collection of the Massachusetts Historical Society, Boston. The National Library, Madrid, possesses the oldest canvas representing Columbus known to exist in Spain. This is the so-called Yanez portrait, which was purchased in 1763 and named in honor of its former owner.

The Marine Museum portrait, here reproduced, was painted probably sometime in the
nineteenth century, and is evidently a composite,
based on these early likenesses, and on data as
to the personal appearance of Columbus gathered from his biographers. Though it possesses no claim to authenticity, it is probably
the most satisfactory representation of the
Columbus of imagination and tradition.

The subject is discussed fully in Volume II
of Justin Winsor's *Narrative and Critical History
of America*.

THE SPANISH CONQUERORS

∵

CHAPTER I

WEST AND EAST

Wherefore we may judge that those persons who connect the region in the neighborhood of the Pillars of Hercules [Spain] with that towards India, and who assert that in this way the sea is ONE, do not assert things very improbable. — ARISTOTLE: *De Cælo*, II, 14.

THE Spaniard of the fifteenth century is recognizable by well-defined traits: he was primitive, he was proud, he was devout, and he was romantic. His primitiveness we detect in his relish for blood and suffering; his pride in his austerity and exclusiveness; his devoutness in his mystical exaltation of the Church; and his romanticism in his passion for adventure.

After printing had spread in Spain, the romanticism of the Spaniard — to confine our observations for the present to that trait — was fostered by a wealth of books. *Amadis of Gaul, Palmerín of England*, *The Exploits of Esplandián*, *Don Beli-anis* — all these works were filled with heroes, queens, monsters, and enchantments; and all, it is needless to remark, held an honored place upon the shelves of Miguel de Cervantes, that Spanish romanticist *par excellence*, the author of *Don Quixote*.

But prior to 1500, or down to 1492, let us say, the romanticism of the Spaniard, like that of other Europeans, was ministered to not so much by books as by tales passed from mouth to mouth: tales originating with seamen and reflected in the names on mariners' charts; and tales by landsmen recorded in the relations, reports, and letters of missionaries, royal envoys, and itinerant merchants.

To the west of Spain stretched the Atlantic Ocean, and in the Atlantic the lands most remote were the Canaries, the Madeiras, the Cape Verde Group, and the Azores. What was beyond the Canaries, the Madeiras, the Cape Verde Group, and the Azores? To this the answer was: "Naught so far as known, save the Atlantic itself — the Mare Tenebrosum or Sea of Darkness; a sea so called for the very reason that within it lies hid whatever land there may be beyond these islands."

West of Ireland but east of the longitude of
the Azores, seamen said, was to be found the island of Brazil; west of the Canaries and also
west of the longitude of the Azores, the great island of Antillia; and southwest of the Cape Verde
Group, at an indeterminate distance, the island of
St. Brandan.   Concerning Brazil, except that the
name signified red or orange-colored dyewood, particulars were lacking; but Antillia — the "island
over against," the "island opposite"— had been
the refuge, had it not, of the Iberian Goths after
their defeat by the Moors; and here two Arch-
bishops of Oporto, with five bishops, had founded
seven cities. St. Brandan, too, was the subject of
somewhat specific affirmation; for in quest of this
island had not St. Brandan, Abbot of Ailach, in
the sixth century put fearlessly to sea with a band
of monks?

Nor were the islands mentioned all of those for
which seamen vouched.   There were, besides, Isla
de Mam (Man Island); Salvagio (Savage Island),
alias La Man de Satanaxio (Hand of Satan); Insula
in Mar (Island in the Sea); Reyella (King Island);
and various others.   Some of these islands, it was
surmised, must be the abode of life; if not life of the
type of the hydras and gorgons of antiquity, at least

of a type extramundane and weird — of Amazons, of men with tails, of "anthropophagi and men whose heads do grow beneath their shoulders," of crouching calibans, of mermaids, and of singing ariels.

And, amid uncertainties respecting Antillia and her protean sisterhood, one certainty stood out: in considerable numbers these islands had figured boldly on marine charts of accepted authority, from the famed "Catalan" of 1375 to the "Beccaria" of 1435, and the "Benincasas" of 1463, 1476, and 1482.

Noteworthy as were the yarns spun by seamen in the fifteenth century, tales circulated by landsmen — by missionaries, royal envoys, and merchants — were more noteworthy still. But these missionaries and other landsmen, whither did they fare? In what quarter did they adventure? Not in the West, for that was the seaman's realm, but in the East these travelers had their domain. The chief potentate in all Asia, so Europe believed, was Prester John, a Christian and a rich man. To find him or some equivalent of him, and bring him into helpful relationship with Christian but distracted Europe, became the ambition of Popes and secular rulers alike. Hence the missionaries. Hence Friar John of Pian de Carpine and Friar William of Rubruck, who from 1245 to 1253 penetrated central Asia to Karakorum. Hence, furthermore, John of Monte Corvino, Odoric of Pordenone, and John of Marignolli, who, as friars and papal legates from 1275 to 1353, visited Persia, India, the Malay Archipelago, China, and even Thibet.

The tales these landsmen brought were good to hear — "pretty to hear tell," as Friar Odoric puts it. First, there was Cathay: Cathay of the Mongol plains, with its kaans or emperors housed in tents, twanging guitars, and disdainful of all mankind; Cathay of the "Ocean Sea" with ports thronged with ships and wharves glutted with costly wares; Cathay of the city of Kinsay — "stretched like Paradise through the breadth of Heaven" — with lake, canals, bridges, pleasure barges, baths, and lights-o'-love; Cathay of imperial Cambulac with its Palace of the Great Kaan, its multitude of crowned barons in silken robes, its magic golden flagons, its troops of splendid white mares, its astrologers, leeches, conjurers, and choruses of girls with "cheeks as full as the moon," who by their "sweet singing" pleased Friar Odoric (ah, Friar!) most of all.

Then there was India, including Cipangu or Japan with its "rose colored pearls" and gold "abundant beyond all measure"; India of the "twenty-four hundred islands and sixty-four crowned kings"; India of the ruby, the sapphire, and the diamond; of the Moluccas drowsy with perfumes and rich in drugs and spices; of the golden temples and the uncouth gods; of the eunuchs and the ivory; the beasts, the serpents, and the brilliant birds. Other tales there were, brought by these landsmen, the missionaries. Just as the West had its Sea of Darkness — the Atlantic Ocean — so the East had its Land of Darkness — the extreme northeast of Asia, a region of mountain and sand, of cold and snow, where dwelt the Gog and Magog of Ezekiel. And to reach this dark land, barriers must be overcome, defiles fierce with demoniac winds, deserts swathed in mystic light and vibrant to jigging tunes, valleys awful with dead men's bones.

Moreover, as in the West the mythical islands of the Dark Sea were the abode of creatures beyond the thought of man, so in the East the Dark Land harbored beings quite as preternatural. Here, co-tenants, so to speak, of Gog and Magog, were the Cynocephalæ or dog-headed creatures;

the Parocitæ so narrow mouthed as to be forced
to subsist exclusively on odors; jointless hopping
creatures who cried "chin chin"; one-eyed creatures; midget creatures; and what not. "I was
told," says Friar Rubruck, "that there is a province beyond Cathay and at whatever age a man
enters it that age he keeps which he had on entering — which," naïvely exclaims the friar, "I do not
believe." Odoric had far more hardihood in narrative, for, speaking of India, he notes: "I heard
tell that there be trees which bear men and women
like fruit upon them . . . [These people] are
fixed in the tree up to the navel and there they be;
when the wind blows they be fresh, but when it
does not blow they are all dried up. This I saw
not in sooth, but I heard it told by people who had
seen it."

As a skeptic among tale-bringers from the East,
however, John of Marignolli ranks foremost. A
Paradise on earth still somewhere existing; an
Adam's footprint in Ceylon; a Noah's Ark still
on Ararat — such things were verities to him; but
not so preternatural creatures. "The truth is,"
he declares, "no such people do exist as nations,
though there may be an individual monster here
and there." Indeed, so adventurous in skepticism

is John that in some particulars he o'erleaps
himself. "There are," he avers, "no Antipodes —
men having the soles of their feet opposite to ours.
Certainly not." He has learned too, "by sure
experience," that "if the ocean be divided by two
lines forming a cross, two of the quadrants so resulting are navigable and the two others not navigable at all, for God willed not that men should
be able to sail round the whole world."

So far as missionaries were concerned, the East
might lure them to Cathay, or even to farthest
India, through interest in some shadowy Prester
John, an interest largely of a religious nature; but
it was otherwise with royal envoys and merchants.
The lure of the East for them was treasure and
merchandise, in other words, wealth. As early
as 1165–67, a Spanish Jew of Navarre, Rabbi Benjamin by name, who was concerned in trade, set
forth from Tudela, his native city, and visiting
Saragossa, Genoa, Constantinople, Tyre, Damas-
cus, Bagdad, and points in Arabia, reached the
island of Kish and the mouth of the Persian Gulf,
at the gates of India and within earshot of Cathay.
He was the first modern European, it is said, "to
as much as mention China."

Nearly a century later (1254) appeared the

royal traveler Heythum I, King of Lesser Armenia, on a visit to Mangu Kaan at Karakorum. Then in 1275 came Marco Polo, son and nephew of traders bred in the commercial traditions of Venice, and himself the first European of parts to tell of the splendors of the Great Kaan. Polo's most interesting successor (1325-55) was an Arab man of the world, gay, selfish, sensuous, and observing, Ibn Batuta. Batuta journeyed deviously from Morocco to Cathay and India. Thence he leisurely returned to his native Tangier by way of Spain; and as he strolled he sang:

> Of all the Four Quarters of Heaven the best
> (I'll prove it past question) is surely the West.[1]

To these landsmen, the envoys and merchants, the lure of the East was wealth. It was silks: silks of Gilán; taffetas of Shiraz, Yezd, and Serpi; "sendels of grene and broun"; cloth of gold, gold bro-

[1] In the fifteenth century two travelers gained celebrity by their narrations: one a Spanish Knight, Ruy Gonzalez of Clavijo; the other a Venetian merchant, Nicolo de' Conti. Gonzalez in 1403 went from Spain, by way of the eastern Mediterranean and Black Seas, which Genoa controlled, to represent Henry III of Castile before Tamerlane the Great at Samarcand — "silken Samarcand" — in Mongolia; while Conti, retracing in part the steps of Rabbi Benjamin, passed (1419-1444) to the mouth of the Persian Gulf and on into the Malay Archipelago.

cades; silver gauze; silks and satins of Su-Chau; cramoisy; fabrics wrought in beasts, birds, trees, and flowers. It was also gold: ingots of gold; beaten gold; gold and silver plate; gold pillars and lamps; gold coronets and headdresses; gold armlets and anklets; gold girdles, cinctures, censers, cups, and basins.

Pearls, too, of "beautiful water" and gems, especially of India, made part of this wealth. Said Ibn Batuta: "Men at Kish descend to the bed of the sea [the Persian Gulf] by ropes and collect shellfish, then split them and extract the pearls." Again he said: "I traversed the bazar of the jewelers at Tabriz, and my eyes were dazzled by the variety of precious stones which I beheld. Handsome slaves, superbly dressed, and girdled with silk, offered their gems for sale to the Tartar ladies who bought great numbers."

But of all this wealth — so luring in the fact, so alluring in the recital — the chief items were aromatics and spices: sandalwood, aloewood, spikenard, frankincense, civet, and musk; rhubarb, nutmegs, mace, cloves, ginger, pepper, and cinnamon. And of spices one stood preëminent — pepper. Rabbi Benjamin was of his time when he said that "two parasangs from the Sea of Sodom is

the Pillar of Salt into which Lot's wife was turned";
but he was for subsequent times, as well, when he
described the pearls and pepper. To the heat of
pepper land, Malabar, a Persian ambassador to
India once bore witness in the statement that so
intense was this heat that "it burned the ruby in
the mine and the marrow in the bones," to say
naught of "melting the sword in the scabbard like
wax." But this by the way. Pepper it was, the
spice which in ancient days had formed part of
the ransom of Rome from Alaric, that throughout
the Middle Ages and far into the fifteenth century
constituted in Europe the commodity most prized
and talked of, for it was the one most costly, the
one closest to gold in intrinsic worth.

Prior to 1492, then, the romanticism of the
Spaniard, as of other Europeans, was stirred by
tales of the West and tales of the East — tales by
seamen and tales by landsmen — and these in the
main were circulated by word of mouth. Furthermore, so potent were these stories that, even
when ascribed to mere weavers of dreams, they
would not be denied and could not be ignored.
And, in the minds of two or three persons, they
begat the old question of Aristotle: "Might not
the Ocean Sea, which bordered Cathay and held

Cipangu, be one with the Sea of Darkness which lay west of Europe and held Antillia?"

THE BEHAIM GLOBE OF 1492
After Kretschmer

CHAPTER II

COLUMBUS AND NEW LANDS

> . . . for my purpose holds
> To sail beyond the sunset, and the baths
> Of all the western stars. . . .
> It may be we shall touch the Happy Isles.
>
> TENNYSON: *Ulysses.*

AMONG sojourners in Spain, prior to 1492, there was a Genoese, by name Christopher Columbus. He was tall and well-built, of dignified mien, with red hair and beard, a long ruddy face, clear gray eyes, and aquiline nose. To inferiors his manner was exacting and brusque, to equals it was urbane, and to superiors it was courtly. His figure showed to advantage, whereof he was not unduly aware, and he evinced a taste for yellow in beads and for crimson and scarlet in caps, cloaks, and shoes.

Unlike the Spaniards, whom he was to lead, Columbus was not in disposition primitive; he had no relish for blood and suffering. He was,

13

however, proud, with a measure of austerity; and he was highly romantic and strikingly devout.

His most signal powers, and they were signal indeed, were moral powers. In patience, endurance, tenacity, energy, will — powers which, far more than those distinctively intellectual, make for greatness — the world has rarely known his equal. Imagination, too, he possessed, rich and ardent, and it rendered him poetic, eloquent, and persuasive. But, just as he possessed the qualities named, so likewise he possessed the defects of them. He was masterful and imaginative, but his masterfulness tended to ungenerousness and his imagination to vagary and mischievous exaggeration. Nor was this all. His moral powers were largely determined in exercise by two positive principles of action which were undeniably sinister — vanity and cupidity — and under stress of these he became at times dissimulating, boastful, and crafty. It is probable, however, that the sinister in him has by recent writers been somewhat over-magnified. Throughout everything he was sincerely and enthusiastically religious. To him, as to others of Machiavellian strain, the end justified many means but not all, though among the justified means were those of guile.

According to the findings of the most recent scholarship, Christopher Columbus, the eldest in a family of four sons and one daughter,[1] was born at Genoa on a date between August 26 and October 31, 1451. His grandfather probably, and his father certainly, was a wool-dealer and weaver; and the latter at one time also conducted a wine-shop. None of his progenitors had place or rank, and his sister married a cheesemonger.   There were other persons in Europe in his time of the sobriquet "Columbus," one of whom, William of Caseneuve, was a corsair and vice-admiral of France under Louis XI; and with these Christopher Columbus, about 1501, sought to indicate relationship by the remark that "he was not the first admiral in his family."   But the claim, so far as can be ascertained, was wanting in foundation.

The education of Christopher was of the most elementary sort.   It consisted merely of what was provided by a school maintained by the weavers' guild of the town of his birth, in a little street called Pavia Lane.   How meager his first advantages were, appears in the fact that at no time in life did he assume to write his mother tongue, Italian, not even when addressing the Bank of St. George in Genoa.

[1] Christopher, Bartholomew, Giovanni, Diego, and Bianchinetta.

We have seen that as a man Columbus was both vigorous of body and imaginative of mind. For him, therefore, as a lad in Genoa — the Genoa of our travelers, Rabbi Benjamin, Marco Polo, and Ibn Batuta — to develop a taste for the sea was more natural than not. In fact, he tells us that from his fourteenth year he was accustomed to embark on ships. But in 1472, when he was twenty-one years old, he declared before a notary that he was by trade a weaver. We may suppose then that up to this period his seafaring was tentative or in the nature of a youth's adventures; thereafter it became more and more an occupation.

In Genoa, at this time, dwelt two noblemen with whom Columbus seems to have been on terms of friendship. He went with them in 1475 to the island of Chios in the Ægean, where he obtained a shipment of malmsey wine, and became familiar with "mastic." In 1476 the two noblemen embarked on a voyage to England, and again Columbus accompanied them in a flotilla — for it was a voyage of importance — which consisted of five armed merchantmen. When they were off Cape St. Vincent, who should appear but the corsair and French vice-admiral, William of Caseneuve, *alias* "Columbus"! Between the Genoese vessels and those of Louis XI there straightway ensued a desperate struggle. In the end, ships on both sides took fire, and the crews leaped overboard. Columbus of Genoa, the future discoverer, leaped with others and, being fortunate enough to be picked up, was landed on the Portuguese coast near Lisbon, wounded, drenched, and exhausted. Such, in August, 1476, was the advent of Columbus in Portugal, an advent certainly fortuitous if not "miraculous," as he terms it.

From Lisbon, Columbus continued in December his interrupted voyage to England, stopping probably at Bristol; and it would seem that he even adventured into the seas toward Iceland. "I sailed," he says, as quoted by his son Ferdinand, "in the month of February, 1477, a hundred leagues beyond the island of Thule [Iceland]." At some period prior to 1503 the discoverer had read the Latin poet Seneca and found the lines:

> In later ages a time shall come,
> When the Ocean shall relax its chains;
> When Tiphys shall disclose new lands,
> And Thule shall no longer be earth's bound.

Now Columbus took Tiphys, the pilot, as his own prototype; and, to make the identification more

2

complete, he may have deemed it well that the discoverer of America should, as a preliminary, have fared beyond Thule.

In the career of Columbus, Portugal was the first turning-point. Hither he returned in 1477 or 1478; and here, in 1479 or 1480, after a trip back to Genoa, he married. This event was the reward of his piety. In Lisbon there was a convent of the religious Order of St. Jacques, called the Convent of Saints. Its protégées were bound to vows of chastity — conjugal chastity, not celibacy — and among them was Felipa, a daughter of two of the noblest of Portuguese houses, and Felipa was beautiful. Coming daily to the chapel of this convent to make his devotions, Columbus saw Felipa, fell in love with her, and they were wed. To the couple, in 1480 or 1481, a child was born — Columbus's first son, Diego. At this period, too, Columbus became associated in Lisbon with his younger brother, Bartholomew, a prepossessing youth of about nineteen, astute, of some education, and skilled in the art of limning marine charts.

The father of Felipa Columbus was Bartholomew Perestrello, Governor of Porto Santo of the Madeira Group, and it is a firm tradition that, at his death in 1457, he left to his wife Isabel, Felipa's mother, charts and papers which served first to direct Columbus's mind toward great projects in the West.   Another tradition — long credited, then long discredited, and now revived — was that Columbus, upon his marriage, settled in the island of Madeira, which is near to that of Porto Santo, and that, while he was here, a Spanish ship, which had been driven westward to the island afterwards found by Columbus and named Española, came forlornly back, getting as far only as Madeira. Here, so the tradition ran, the pilot of the ship, together with such of the crew as survived, debarked; but the crew, famished and sick, all died, leaving only the pilot.   Then he, too, died in the house of Columbus; but not before he had imparted to his host the amazing story of his voyage and had given to him his log and a chart of his route.

Be the truth of these two traditions what it may, it is a well-settled fact that in Portugal Columbus met pilots and captains and was enabled to accompany Portuguese expeditions down the coast of Africa.   "I was," he says, "at the Fortress of St. George of the Mine, belonging to the King of Portugal, which lies below the equinoctial line."   The object of such voyages was largely the discovery of new islands. The Canaries and the Madeiras, the outermost of the Azores and the Cape Verde Group, all were treasure-trove of the fifteenth century, and there might well be others. In these times, indeed, islands rose smiling to greet the discoverer on his approach. Nay more: where actual islands were not forthcoming, imaginary ones developed in their stead. But were these isles as mythical and imaginary as they were represented? The question is pertinent, for upon the answer depends in good measure what we shall think of the nature of the incentive which underlay the voyage of 1492, the voyage resulting in the discovery of America.

The very appearance of islands like Antillia, Salvagio, Reyella, and Insula in Mar on charts such, for example, as the "Beccaria" of 1435 attests the prevalence of a tradition — and that a mature one — that such a group existed. Such a tradition could probably have had but one origin: chance voyages across the Atlantic from Europe to North America, and especially to the West India Islands of North America. Indeed, in 1474 or 1475, Fernão Telles sought the mythical Antillia — sometimes called the Isle of the Seven Cities —

under express warrant from the King of Portugal, Alfonso V. And in his journal of 1492 Columbus records that "many honorable Spanish gentlemen [of the Canary Group] declared that every year they saw land to the west of the Canaries." Again he records that in 1484, when he was in Portugal, "a man [Domimguez do Arco] came to the King [John II] from the Island of Madeira to beg for a caravel to go to this island that was seen"; and that "the same thing [the existence of an island in the West] was affirmed in the Azores." How, therefore, there might arise a story, true or false, of a shipwrecked pilot who gave to Columbus the clue to the finding of the island of Española, may readily be perceived. But, concerning stories of and by pilots, more anon.

Columbus had now acquired some knowledge of the theory and art of navigation, and, incidentally, some knowledge of Latin; and having made up his mind, as had Telles before him, that in the Atlantic to the west there yet remained "islands and lands" to be discovered, he obtained an audience with the King of Portugal and laid before him a definite proposal. He asked for three caravels equipped and supplied for a year; and, in the event of lands being found, for the viceroyalty and perpetual government therein, a tenth of the income therefrom, the rank of nobleman, and the title of grand admiral.

According to Portuguese chroniclers writing in the sixteenth century, the particular "land" Columbus had in view was Cipangu or Japan. But, whatever Columbus may have disclosed or reserved with respect to Japan, or with respect to Antillia, at this first interview with the Portuguese King, so affronted was the monarch by what he felt to be the vanity and presumption of the petitioner that he promptly referred his plea to a council of three experts, by whom, after some deliberation, it was dismissed. Thereupon Columbus, late in 1485 or early in 1486, left Portugal for Spain.

At this point in the fortunes of Christopher Columbus, there arises for consideration a peculiar circumstance. Columbus had a double, the well-known cosmographer of Nuremberg, Martin Behaim. Like Columbus, this man was born near the middle of the fifteenth century; like him, he lacked university training; like him, his early activities were commercial; like him, he settled in Portugal (1480–84); like him, he voyaged to Africa; like him, he was identified with an Atlantic island,

Fayal in his case, and married the daughter of the Governor; like him, he was busied with nautical studies in Lisbon; like him, he was not highly regardful of veracity; and finally, like him, he died in neglect early in the sixteenth century. Behaim, however, unlike Columbus, was of patrician ancestry, was instructed in the use of nautical instruments, became a Knight of Portugal, and at Lisbon had the *entrée* to aristocratic and scientific circles.

The extent of his geographical knowledge may be inferred from a globe which he completed at Nuremberg in 1492, before the return of Columbus from his first voyage. His authorities included Aristotle and Strabo, Ptolemy, Marco Polo, and Sir John Mandeville; but his chief authority was Pierre d'Ailly, whose *Imago Mundi* [World Survey], written in 1410, formed a compendium of the geographical and cosmographical notions of authors such as Marinus of Tyre and Alfraganus the Arabian. To put the matter briefly, the ideas of Pierre d'Ailly and Marco Polo are strikingly expressed in this globe, which shows Cathay and India, both marked rich, opposite to Portugal and Africa, and about 120° west of the Cape Verde Islands and the Azores instead of the actual distance

of over 200°.   Cathay is thus brought forward
nearly to the position of California; Cipango
[Cipangu] or Japan, marked as especially rich,
falls athwart the position of Mexico; while Antillia
lies northeast of the position of Hayti or Española;
and St. Brandan occupies, in part, the position of
northern South America.

But why did Behaim take pains to construct a
globe? The answer is clear. He had recently (1486)
adventured in a project to confirm his geographical
ideas; he had attempted a secret voyage westward
to Asia in partnership with two fellow islanders —
Fernam Dulmo of Terceira, a navigator, and João
Affonso Estreito of Madeira, his patron.   The enterprise had failed; and yet he did not wish his ideas
to be lost or appropriated by another.

Concerning Columbus, however, the important
question is: Was he indebted to Behaim for his
own ideas of cosmography — for the idea, especially, of a small earth? It would hardly seem
so. The two men may have met in Portugal, but,
even if they had, each at the time was guarding a
secret, or the approaches to one: Columbus, that
of islands — perchance of a specific island — to
be discovered; and Behaim, that of a scheme for
exploiting Asia.   That not very much confidential

communication between them was likely under the circumstances may be conjectured.[1]

Columbus, according to his own statement, entered Spain after fourteen years spent in vain labors in Portugal. As a matter of fact, his stay there did not at the utmost exceed ten years, probably only five or six. He came accompanied by his son Diego, for Felipa, beautiful daughter of the Convent of Saints, had probably died soon after Diego's birth. Furthermore, he quitted Portugal, for what reason may never be known, "secretly at night."

In Spain Columbus's first objective was Palos. Here, at the monastery of La Rábida, whose guardian, Antonio de Marchena, the future discoverer is said to have known in Portugal, he found lodgings for himself and a temporary home for his son.

[1] Until within recent years, it was the unquestioned belief that the views regarding the proximity of eastern Asia to western Europe, which Columbus is known to have come to entertain, were due to a letter sent him, about 1480, by Paolo Toscanelli, a distinguished Florentine astronomer. The letter was accompanied, so it was claimed, by a chart of the confronting European and Asiatic seaboards, which Toscanelli himself had drafted, showing Antillia and Japan as, so to speak, halting points or stepping-stones across the intervening Atlantic Ocean. But the belief in a Toscanelli letter no longer is unquestioned. Consult the writings of Vignaud and of Bourne, mentioned on page 219.

The supposition is that at Palos, which as a sea-port was the resort of mariners and where there were many Portuguese, Columbus counted upon obtaining special information with regard to the landfall of some particular early voyage or voyages into the West.

But if Palos was Columbus's first objective in Spain, his second was the Court of the Spanish sovereigns, Ferdinand and Isabella. To these personages Columbus worked his way, so to speak, by the influence of the Duke of Medina Cœli, who had wealth; and who at first contemplated assuming in the schemes of Columbus a rôle not unlike that of Estreito in the project of Behaim. But, coming to realize that the affair was one to be accomplished successfully only under royal patronage, the Duke applied to the sovereigns, who commanded that Columbus himself be sent to Court.

Cordova now for some time had been the seat of government, and here Columbus arrived on January 20, 1486. The sovereigns were then absent, but returned at the end of April or first of May, and the coveted audience took place. What occurred is not known. Presumably Ferdinand and Isabella, after a courteous hearing, smilingly put by the question of exploration, for they referred it to the

Queen's confessor, Hernando de Talavera, an ecclesiastic by no means ungenerous or bigoted, with instructions to summon a council for its consideration. As for the council, not a soul who was a member ever revealed aught of its composition or doings, save Dr. Rodrigo de Maldonado, who says that men of science and mariners were in attendance, no less than literary men and theologuos, and that Columbus himself was subjected to interrogation.

Talavera's council conferred at intervals for five years, often at Salamanca, and at length, late in 1490, reported adversely for Columbus, and the sovereigns accepted the report. In the life of the great Italian adventurer, our future discoverer and admiral, these five years are among the most interesting and significant. They mark, it is true, a moral and material decline, but, like the first years in Portugal, they mark an intellectual advance.

While awaiting action by the council, Columbus was retained at Court and encouraged by occasional donations of money — donations appearing on record as made to "a stranger occupied with certain affairs relative to the service of their Highnesses." The sums, in all, came to $510 (170,000 maravedis); but, small as they were, they had altogether ceased by 1488. In that year it was, or at the end of 1487, the preceding year, that Columbus for a second time fell victim to feminine attractions. The maiden, like his first bride Felipa, was young — eighteen or twenty years old — possessed a beautiful name, Beatrix Enríquez, and doubtless a beautiful person, but, unlike Felipa, she was humble of birth and very poor. So lowly, indeed, was she that Columbus did not stoop to take her in marriage, but formed with her a *liaison*, the result of which was the birth, about August 15, 1488, of his second son and future biographer, Ferdinand.

Between the date just given and the spring of 1489, Columbus would seem to have gone back to Portugal under a safe-conduct from John II, but why he went, if he did go, is unknown, and by May 12, 1489, he was again in Spain and in attendance upon Ferdinand and Isabella at the siege of Baza. Thenceforth, however, until the final rejection of his project by the sovereigns in 1490, he drops from view, excepting as we are accorded glimpses of him gaining bread for himself and Beatrix in Cordova by limning marine charts, wherein he evidently had been instructed by his brother Bartholomew, and by selling printed books. This vending of printed books may have meant much in that intellectual advance which has been spoken of as characterizing for the discoverer-to-be the days, somber or hectic, through which he was now passing.

Some years before his brother had fallen on hard times, Bartholomew Columbus had betaken himself from Portugal (where he had witnessed the return of the great Portuguese captain, Bartholomeu Días, from his discovery of the Cape of Good Hope) to enlist the aid of King Henry VII of England in his brother Christopher's project. Then, abandoning England, he had recourse in turn to France, and now was making himself agreeable at the Court of Charles VIII.

Thither Columbus determined to follow him, but his departure was prevented by a visit which he paid to Palos and to the monastery of La Rábida, to make further arrangements for the care of his son Diego. This visit, unlike the first, does not seem to have been inspired by a specific wish for light upon voyages, with strange landfalls, under strange pilots. Columbus was poverty-stricken and, for once, discouraged. With what cheer he might, he met his friend, the former guardian,

Antonio de Marchena, and also (perhaps for the first time) the officiating guardian, Juan Pérez, once confessor to Queen Isabella.

By these three, under the stimulating zeal of the monks, a plan was contrived. Columbus should thoroughly canvass the maritime section having Palos for a center, for all possible information regarding pioneer voyages into the Sea of Darkness. The first seaman to be sought out and catechized was Pedro de Velasco, a pilot of Palos itself. Next, after Velasco, an unnamed pilot of the port of Santa María, near Cadiz, was visited. He had sailed west from Ireland, and had, he thought, sighted the coasts of Tartary — not improbably Labrador. Finally a second pilot domiciled in Palos, Pedro Vásquez de la Frontera, was waited upon, and what was gathered from him was suggestive indeed. Between 1460 and 1475 he had made a voyage into the West, with "a Prince of Portugal," to discover "new lands." Their purpose was to sail "straight West," but, encountering that vast field of marine herbage known as the Sargasso Sea, he had turned back.

At this time, in Palos, the most important man of maritime affairs was the head of the family of Pinzón — Martín Alonso, "best-known and bravest of captains and pilots" — and to him Columbus would first have addressed himself, had not this mariner been absent with a cargo of sardines at Rome. As it was, Columbus awaited his return eagerly.

Pinzón, as it chanced, was at this juncture cherishing a project of his own for exploring to the West, and while in Rome had sought light at the library of Pope Innocent VIII upon "lands in the Ocean Sea." There he had seen "a map and a book," both of which (in the form of copies, no doubt) he had brought with him. These documents, according to Pinzón's son, Pinzón the father not only submitted to Columbus but gave into his hands. Furthermore Pinzón and Columbus now went together to the house of Pedro Vásquez de la Frontera and got him to repeat the tale of how, with a Prince of Portugal, he had sailed west as far as the Sargasso Sea, from before which he had recoiled. It was necessary "to brave this obstacle," said Vásquez, because by not doing so the Prince had failed to find land. If, on meeting the Sargasso Sea, one would but keep "straight on," it would be "impossible that land should not be found."

How, on his voyage in 1492, Columbus made use

of "a chart" whereon he himself had depicted "certain islands"; how this chart was passed back and forth between him and Martín Alonso Pinzón; and how, apropos of the impending landfall, one of the pilots spoke to Columbus of indications from "your book," are incidents well known. Nor is it less well known that on this voyage, after encountering the Sargasso Sea, Columbus despite protest "braved the obstacle" and kept "straight on," literally "on and on," following as nearly as he could the twenty-eighth parallel, till land rewarded his perseverance.

Not long after the return of Martín Alonso Pinzón from Rome, Guardian Juan Pérez, and perhaps Pinzón also, wrote to Queen Isabella, asking a further hearing for Columbus and his project. The request was granted, and Pérez was summoned to Court at Santa Fé, before Granada. He set out in a manner truly Columbian, alone, on a mule, secretly at low midnight. He was soon empowered to invite Columbus to join him. In December the latter came. Ferdinand and Isabella were in receptive mood. Granada was about to fall and Spain to be delivered from the Moor forever. A council was ordered — one, like Talavera's, composed of philosophers, astrologers, cosmographers,

seamen, and pilots. With Talavera's council, however, the primary consideration had been the theo-
retical feasibility of Columbus's project. With
the new council, it was the practical question of
ways and means that gave pause.

Columbus, repeating with emphasis the terms
submitted to King John II of Portugal, demanded
of Ferdinand and Isabella a patent of nobility,
the admiralty of the ocean, the viceroyalty and
government of all lands discovered, and "a commission of ten per cent upon everything within
the limits of his admiralty which might be bought,
exchanged, found, or gained."   That, in addition,
he should demand three caravels, to cost possibly
2,000,000 maravedis ($6000), was by comparison
trifling.

In after years the discoverer of America was
wont to complain that in his struggle for recognition in Spain "everybody had derided him, save
two monks," Marchena and Pérez.   Derided he
no doubt was, but the cause perhaps was not so
much his belief in problematical islands and lands
as his demand for rewards — rewards which, if
granted, would raise him to a dizzy height, to a
point of rank, power, and riches next to that of the
throne itself.

3

As in 1486, so in 1492, in the month of January
to which we are now come, Columbus was dismissed a second time from the Spanish Court
and departed sorrowing. The royal flags streamed
from the towers of the Alhambra, for Granada had
fallen, but in this event our Genoese took little
interest. His course led him toward Cordova, for
here was Beatrix Enríquez with Ferdinand, now
in his fourth year; and here must now be brought
Diego, ten or twelve years old, from La Rábida.
Again it must have been France, his last hope
among the nations, with which the thoughts of
Columbus were busy. Be that as it may, when but
two leagues from Granada who should overtake
him but a royal constable, sent posthaste by the
Queen with orders for his return! His demands,
one and all, would be complied with.

What specifically it was that induced the Spanish
sovereigns to change their minds may be only inferred. Whether it was proof of actual islands to
the west, proof secretly confided to Columbus at
Palos, no one knows. Whatever it was, the lost
cause was powerfully pleaded before Isabella by
Luis de Santangel, treasurer of Aragon; and before
Ferdinand by Juan Cabrero, his chamberlain, and
by Juan Diego of Deza, preceptor to Prince John.

The risk was small, the possibilities for God and the realm were incalculable — such, we are told, was the reasoning. Especially was it the reasoning of Santangel; and so wrought upon by it was Isabella, that, seized with enthusiasm, she is said to have tendered her jewels, priceless gems that they were, in security for money for the enterprise. [1]

What manner of navigator was this Genoese, this Christopher Columbus, by whom this vast enterprise had been conceived, and by whom it

---

[1] But just here a question. Columbus knew that the world was round, and, like Behaim his double, had read Ser Marco Polo's Book and the *Travels of Sir John Mandeville*. Unlike Behaim, however, he in all probability had not read the *Imago Mundi* of Pierre d'Ailly, with its doctrine of a small earth, and hence of a short route to Asia. Is it likely, then, that in 1492 his objective was Asia, as was Behaim's in 1486? Is it not more likely that it was merely "islands and lands" in the far Atlantic?

And again. In 1492, on the 17th of April, the Spanish sovereigns issued to Columbus a Capitulation empowering him, on his own terms, to seek "islands and lands" but in no way mentioning Asia; and this Capitulation was confirmed by Letters Patent on the 30th of April. Now may not the failure here to mention Asia, (Cathay or India) be due to a fact — the fact, namely, that Columbus's hopes and expectations stopped short of Asia?

One might perhaps think that the aims of Columbus were exclusive of Asia, were it not for two considerations: the first, that he had cause, both from Marco Polo's Book and from Pinzón personally, to be aware that Asia was a background to Japan, and, like it, probably attainable from the West; the second, that in 1492 he carried with him, besides a general passport, a special "Letter" from his sovereigns to "The Most Serene Prince, our very dear friend," etc. — a document almost certainly implying the Great Kaan of Cathay.

a longer unbroken voyage than they really were. He, in fact, states repeatedly, in his *Journal*, that he kept a dual reckoning, one of actual distances for himself and one of minimized distances for his men.   How he could have contrived to do this, with half a dozen pilots and a score or more of others at his elbow more competent at rating a ship's progress than himself, "goodness," as Lord Dunraven puts it, "only knows."

A landfall, in the case of any fifteenth century voyage of discovery, was momentous, but especially was it so in the case of a Spanish voyage. Commanders fell on their knees and gave thanks; crews chanted the *Gloria in Excelsis Deo* and crowded into the rigging and tops; flags were run up and guns were fired.   So was it at Guanahani on October 12, 1492.   Clad in armor, over which, true to his taste in color and to his instinct for effect, he had thrown the crimson robe of an Admiral of Castile, Columbus, with the furled royal standard grasped in his left hand, bent low to the earth, which he saluted.   His actions were imitated by the captains of the *Pinta* and *Niña*, Martín Alonso Pinzón and his brother Vicente Yañes, who bore standards emblazoned each with a green cross. Then, rising, Columbus summoned to him the royal

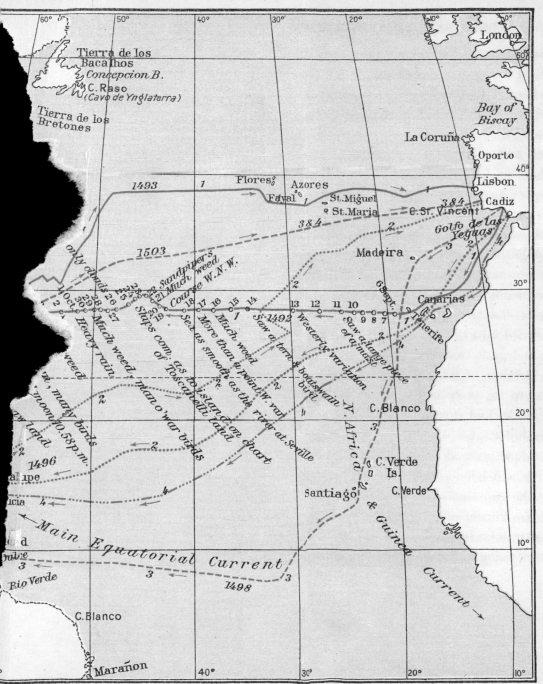

Tierra de los Bacalhos
Concepcion B.
C. Raso
(Cavo de Ynglaterra)

Tierra de los Bretones

London

Bay of Biscay

La Coruña

Oporto

1493   1   Flores   Azores   Lisbon
Fayal   1   St. Miguel   Cadiz
St. Maria   C. St. Vincent
3 & 4   3 & 4
Golfo de las Yeguas
2   3
1503   1
only clouds   Madeira   Canarias
28 sandpipers   Much weed   30°
14 Oct.   21 Much weed   Course W.N.W.
2   31 30 29 28 26 25 24 23   6 Sept.
27   22   Tenerife
19 20   18   17 16 15 14   13 12 11 10   Saw a strange piece
Ships com: as to island on   9 8 7   of a mast
Heavy rain   Much weed   1   1492   Saw a strange piece
Much weed, man o'war birds   More than a point W. var   Westerly variation   Tenerife
Sea as smooth as the river at Seville   Saw a tern & a boatswain   N. Africa   C. Blanco
Toscanelli land   bird   2
m, many birds   2   4   3
moon 10.58 p.m.   C. Verde Is.
Saw land   C. Verde
1496   2   4   Santiago   & Guinea Current
alupe   4
icia   4

Main Equatorial Current
3
Rio Verde   3   4
1498   3

C. Blanco

Marañon   40°   30°   20°   10°

JULIUS BIEN LITH. N.Y.

THE FOUR VOYAGES
OF
COLUMBUS
1492-1503

Based on a map in Bourne's "Spain in America"
(American Nation Series, Vol.3, Harpers, New York, 1904)

———————— 1st voyage 1492-93
·············· 2nd voyage 1495-96
– – – – – 3rd voyage 1498-1500
–·–·–·–· 4th voyage 1502-03

Gulf Stre

Guanahani

Duck's seen overhead

Ducks seen at night

Saw a green rush & a pole, thought right

Cuba

Espa- ñola

Jamaica

I. de los Pinos

Gracias á Dios

S. Juan

MAR DEL NORTE

C. de la Vela

G. de Venezuela

La Huerta

Belén

Margarita

Cumaná

Urabá

MAR DEL SUR

PREPARED FOR THE CHRONICLES OF AMERICA UNDER THE
DIRECTION OF W.L.G.JOERG, AMERICAN GEOGRAPHICAL SOCIETY

notary and the royal inspector as witnesses, unfurled the royal standard, drew his sword, and
proclaimed the island the possession henceforth of
the Crown of Spain, naming it San Salvador.

So the day ended; but early the next morning,
as we are told, the natives gathered on the shore in
large numbers, and, destitute of beards themselves,
looked with wonder on the bearded Spaniards, or
Columbus in particular.   To his beard and those
of his men they "reached out their fingers, and
viewed attentively the whiteness of the Spanish
hands and faces."

On the 28th of October the expedition discovered
Cuba, and on the 5th of December, Hayti or
Española.   Everywhere Columbus was charmed
with the scenery.   "The herbage is like that of
April in Andalusia."   Andalusia serves always as
the standard of comparison.   So pleasant are the
songs of birds that "it seems as though a man could
never wish to leave the place."   Parrots rise in
"flocks so dense as to conceal the sun."   In Cuba
are "palm trees differing from those in Spain and
Guinea."   As for the inhabitants of the new regions, they are "docile," "very gentle and kind,"
going "naked without arms and without law."   But
the things which make a particular appeal to the

discoverer are five: gold, religion, spices, Cipangu, and Cathay.

Gold he began inquiring about from the natives on the day following the landing. "I was attentive and took trouble to ascertain," he says, "if there was gold." But gold, in the *Journal*, is a theme hardly more emphasized than religion. On the very day of the landing Columbus writes: "I believe that they [the natives] would easily be made Christians as it appeared to me they had no sect."

He was equally attentive to any mention of spices. "According as I obtain tidings of gold or spices, I shall settle what must be done." Moreover it is in connection with spices that the *Journal* introduces Cipangu and Cathay. Having, on the 7th of October, given over the search for the "mainland," Columbus on the 21st speaks of proceeding to Cipangu, which he identifies with Cuba because of the latter's "size and riches." It is better, he says, to "inspect much land until some very profitable country is reached, my belief being that it will be rich in spices." And on the 24th he resumes: "On the spheres that I saw [before leaving Spain], and on the paintings of world-maps, Cipangu is in this region." Then,

on the 26th of October, the subject is dropped
with the remark: "I departed . . . for Cuba, for,
by the signs the Indians made of its greatness and
of its gold and pearls, I thought that it must be the
one — that is to say, Cipangu."

But, the mainland recurs in his thoughts; and
on the 30th he decides, from a statement by the
Indians, that Cuba itself is the mainland of Asia,
with Cathay and the Great Kaan somewhere
therein; and that he must send to the latter the
credentials he bears from Ferdinand and Isabella.
Accordingly, on the 2d of November, he dis-
patches from a point on the Cuban coast his official interpreter, Luis de Torres, a converted Jew,
with a party carrying "specimens of spices," to
"ask for the King of that land." To him they are
to deliver the credentials, and from him they are
to inquire "concerning certain provinces, ports,
and rivers, of which the Admiral has notice."

Later, Columbus identified Cipangu with Hayti;
but Cuba he consistently continued to regard as
the mainland, peering expectantly into its bays
and up its streams for "populous cities" such as
the Kinsay of Marco Polo and of the world
maps, maps like Fra Mauro's of 1457–59, which he
"saw" before leaving Spain. Having completed

his voyage by "finding what he sought," though manifestly not "populous cities," Columbus set sail from the eastern end of the island of Hayti for home on January 16, 1493.

Two occurrences hastened his return. On November 21, 1492, Martín Alonso Pinzón, impatient for the discovery of Cipangu and the realization of those dreams of gold on the strength of which he had secured enlistments at Palos, had gone off in the *Pinta* for some prospecting of his own. Then, on Christmas night, the *Santa María* had been wrecked, leaving the Admiral with only the *Niña* wherein to continue his explorations. Thus handicapped, he had been forced to build on Española (Hayti) a fortress, La Navidad, where he left thirty-seven of his men, and crowded into the *Niña* the remainder.

Pinzón had rejoined the expedition on January 6, 1493, but the Admiral was much vexed and not disposed to parley or linger. Nor is his vexation hard to understand. Columbus was the titular and technical head of the expedition, but in reality he was much the servant of his lieutenant, for Pinzón was a Spaniard, the friend and fellow-townsman of the crews, who would not have endured to see him disciplined.

In strong contrast to the voyage out, the voyage back was tempestuous. Storms began on the 12th of February and so grew in violence that on the 14th Columbus placed in a barrel a parchment inscribed with an account of his discoveries and committed it to the sea. But he succeeded in making port in the Portuguese island of Santa María, one of the Azores, whence he sailed for Castile. More storms delayed him, but on the 4th of March the *Niña* entered the Tagus and anchored off Rastelo. Of the fate of the *Pinta*, meanwhile, nothing had been known since the 14th of February, when she had disappeared running before the wind.

Once at anchor, and once having satisfied the Portuguese authorities that he was a duly accredited officer of the Spanish Marine, Columbus was hospitably received, granted supplies, and invited by King John II, the same with whom he had held memorable converse in 1483 or 1484, to visit him at Valparaíso near Lisbon. Columbus went with some trepidation and, according to Portuguese accounts, told the King that he "had come from the discovery of the islands of Cipangu and Antillia," but made no mention of Cathay and the Great Kaan, or of India. "O man of

4

miserable understanding," the King is said, by
Spaniards, to have exclaimed at the interview,
smiting his breast, "why didst thou let an undertaking of such great importance go out of thine
hands!"

By the 15th of March the Admiral was at Palos,
where on the evening of the same day Martín Alonso
Pinzón likewise arrived, having brought the *Pinta*
safe into port at Bayona in Galicia. But it was a full
month before Columbus was received by Ferdinand
and Isabella in Barcelona, and in the meantime Pinzón, already ill when he disembarked, had breathed
his last. What light upon the great voyage to the
Antilles might have been shed had Pinzón — force-
ful personality that he was — survived!

In Sevilla where, amid much ovation, Columbus
awaited the pleasure of the Spanish sovereigns,
there came to him a letter, dated the 30th of
March, addressed to "The Admiral of the Ocean
Sea and Viceroy and Governor of the islands discovered in the Indies," and confirming what had
previously been conditionally granted to him in the
Capitulation and Letters Patent of April, 1492.

If the welcome to the Admiral at Sevilla had
been noteworthy, that which he was accorded at
Barcelona was more noteworthy still. Throngs

attended him, and his bodyguard was the best chivalry of Spain. In advance marched a group of some half-dozen New World Indians and a squad of sailors from the *Niña*. The Indians wore gold armaments and carried spears and arrows, while the sailors bore aloft forty parrots of gorgeous plumage, besides other birds, together with rare plants and animals, among which not the least was an Iguana five feet long, its back bristling with spines.

Ferdinand and Isabella, happy at the success of their adventurous protégé, which no doubt they had scarcely expected, were augustly gracious. Seated under a golden canopy in the Alcázar of the Moorish Kings, they rose to greet Columbus on his entry, gently deprecated his lowliness in stooping to kiss their hands, and made him sit at their feet. So placed, the discoverer of America, a master of speech, told his tale, illustrating it with the Indians, the sailors, the specimens, and the gold. The monarchs and court then said a prayer, the choir of the royal chapel chanted *Te Deum*, and the ceremony closed.

The news of the return of Columbus soon spread and evoked ingenious appraisals among the learned. "In the month of August last," as Hannibal

Januarius, an Italian gentleman from Barcelona, wrote to his brother in 1493: "This great King [Ferdinand], at the prayer of one named Collomba, caused four [*sic*] little vessels to be equipped to navigate . . . upon the ocean in a straight line toward the west until finally the east was reached. The earth being round he should certainly arrive in the eastern regions."   Also from Barcelona, on the 14th of May, Peter Martyr, the Horace Walpole of his day, wrote to his friend Count Tindilla: "A few days after [an attempted assassination of King Ferdinand], there returned from the Western Antipodes a certain Christopher Columbus, a Ligurian, who with barely three ships penetrated to the province which was believed to be fabulous: he returned bearing substantial proofs in the shape of many precious things and particularly of gold."   Again, on the 1st of October, this time from Milan, Martyr wrote to the Archbishop of Braga: "A certain Columbus has sailed to the Western Antipodes, even as he believes to the very shores of India. He has discovered many islands beyond the eastern ocean adjoining the Indies, which are believed to be those of which mention has been made among cosmographers. I do not wholly deny this, although the magnitude of the

globe seems to suggest otherwise, for there are not
wanting those who think it but a small journey
from the end of Spain to the shores of India."
Finally, on January 31, 1494, our letter-writer
addresses these words to the Archbishop of Granada: "The King and Queen at Barcelona have
created an Admiral of the Ocean Sea, Columbus
returned from his most honorable charge, and they
have admitted him to sit in their presence, which is,
as you know, a supreme proof of benevolence and
honor with our Sovereigns."

But, anticipating rumors, reports, and letters,
Columbus himself had had a word to say respecting his voyage. Writing from shipboard, on February 15, 1493, to Luis de Santangel, his stanch
advocate with Isabella, he had declared: "When
I reached Juana [Cuba] I followed its coast west-
wardly and found it so large that I thought it
might be the mainland province of Cathay."

As a matter of fact, however, interest in this
exploit on the part of Columbus attached itself less
to the geographical discoveries than to the preternatural creatures that lurked on the margins of the
earth. Hannibal Januarius, our Italian acquaintance of epistolary bent, remarked to his brother,

apropos of the Genoese navigator, that "the earth being round the latter should certainly arrive in the eastern regions." But forgetful, near the end of his letter, of the scientific aspects of the great voyage, Januarius wrote: "He [Columbus] adds that he has lately been in a country where men are born with tails." Nor was the soft impeachment wholly inaccurate, for, in his own shipboard letter to Santangel, the Admiral said: "There remains for me on the western side [of Cuba] two provinces whereto I did not go — one of which they call Anan — where the people are born with tails." And in his *Journal* Columbus had already noted that "far away" there were, as he understood, "men with one eye, and others with dogs' noses who were cannibals." But he was wary in statement, for in the Santangel letter he concluded the subject by remarking that "down to the present [he had] not found in those islands [the Antilles] any monstrous men as many expected."

With regard to mermaids it was different. These the Admiral had himself seen, both on the coast of Guinea and in the Antilles. The Antillean sirens, as he had seen them, were three in number. "They rose well out of the sea" but were "not so beautiful as painted, though having to some extent the human face." And Columbus believed in Amazons. He had never beheld any, but had been told they lived in the island of Martinino [Martinique], and he had meant to stop there on his way home to secure a few to exhibit, along with his Indians, to Ferdinand and Isabella.

His half-dozen Indians, his forty gorgeous parrots, his spined iguana, and his gold — of the latter not more than enough to whet a royal appetite — together with stories about "mermaids," and natives who burnt a queer herb, "tabacos," were about all in the way of wonders, ocular or auricular, that Columbus had brought home with him. The great thing, the super-epochmaking thing, though not yet understood so to be, was the voyage itself; the voyage itself and the will to make it. This, too, largely irrespective of whether the objective was in some sort Asia, or simply a Barataria, an island to govern.

Besides the voyage of 1492, Columbus made three other voyages. On the second, which lasted from September, 1493, to March, 1496, and was undertaken with seventeen ships and fifteen hundred men, including his brother Diego, he discovered Porto Rico and Jamaica; learned that his colony of 1492 at La Navidad had been totally destroyed; and founded in its stead, in Española (Hayti), the ambitious settlement of Isabella. He also visited Cuba and compelled his entire ships' company to make oath that they believed it to be the mainland, the Alpha or beginning of the Indies.

The third voyage of Columbus from January, 1498, to October, 1500, was undertaken with six ships and two hundred men, to test the opinion of King John II of Portugal that to the south there lay a continent; and the opinion was sustained, for the voyage was signalized by the Admiral's greatest achievement next to that of 1492 — the discovery of the mainland of America, at Paria, near the mouths of the Orinoco. Mistaking the land at first for an insular body, he soon came to realize its true character. As early as July, 1498, he wrote: "It is certain that the discovery of this land in this place is as great a miracle as the discovery on the first voyage"; and in August he thus confided to his *Journal:* "I am convinced that this is the mainland, and very large, of which no knowledge has been had until now." Later, in October, when writing to Ferdinand and Isabella, he said: "I think that if the river mentioned [the Orinoco] does not proceed from the terrestrial paradise, it comes from an immense tract of land in the South, of which no knowledge has been hitherto obtained."

But meanwhile in Española conditions, social, political, and economical, had become chaotic; and in 1500 the Admiral was superseded as Governor by Francisco de Bobadilla, who, stretching his authority, arrested his predecessor, together with his brother Bartholomew and his brother Diego, and sent them to Spain in fetters. Promptly released by the sovereigns, Columbus, after an affecting and (on his part, we may be sure) eloquent scene with Isabella, was released with the promise of a restoration of his privileges as defined in the Capitulation and Letters Patent and was placed, so to speak, on waiting orders.

By 1501 the Admiral had conceived the project of a fourth voyage, to be made with four caravels and one hundred and fifty men; but before setting out, in 1502, he deposited his papers in safe keeping, drafted his will, and wrote to the Bank of St. George in Genoa, offering a tenth of his yearly income for the reduction of food taxes in that commonwealth. This last maritime enterprise was shared by his brother Bartholomew and his son Ferdinand, now a lad of fourteen, and had for its main motive the disclosure of some avenue by which Asia — that part of it where lay the riches — might be attained. In short, Columbus had now come to realize that thus far he had failed to reach the country of the Great Kaan. He felt that he must have reached Asia, but at a point lying to the south of Cathay and India; and, as for flanking the difficulty by penetrating to the south yet further, an immense tract of land, "a mainland," interposed. Still, in the interposing mass there must be a narrow place, and through this a strait, for the currents that set westward from Jamaica so indicated. It is to be observed that on this voyage he pretty much ceased to concern himself with Cipangu, so manifestly futile were all attempts to identify it with Española.

For a full year Columbus skirted the coast of Central America from Cariari in Nicaragua to the site of Puerto Bello in Panamá, hearing of "pepper" and of people in "rich clothing," of commerce, and of the "river Ganges." In November, 1504, he returned to Spain, where Isabella, his patroness, was at this time ‘on her death-bed, so that his many letters to the Spanish Court remained unacknowledged.

With some premonition of his own demise, Columbus now busied himself with his last will, charging his son Diego to provide for the maintenance of Beatrix, "a person to whom I am under great obligations; and let this," he continues, "be done for the discharge of my conscience, for it weighs heavy on my soul." On May 20, 1506, at Valladolid, broken, discouraged, and well-nigh forgotten even in Spain, the discoverer of America, Viceroy of the Indies, and Admiral of the Ocean, breathed his last.

The discoverer of America strikingly illustrates the aphorism that the world's great men, so far from having commonly been men of learning, have often been but glorified enthusiasts. To Columbus the South, the upper coast of South America at the mouths of the Orinoco, meant the Terrestrial Paradise of Sir John Mandeville, a spot where the earth's surface ceasing to be rounded was pinched into a stem, on the summit of which the Paradise rested, and down the sides of which rolled such mighty streams as the Orinoco. It meant also the Golden Chersonese of Ptolemy (Malay Peninsula), where in one year Solomon gathered 656 quintals of gold and all manner of precious stones. It was because of this South, so gravely misconceived by him geographically, that Columbus, anticipating the project of Magellan, entertained at the end of his second voyage the idea of returning to Europe by way of the Indian Ocean. "If he had had an abundance of provisions," says his son Ferdinand, "he would not have returned to Spain except by way of the East."

To say of Columbus that he was not conspicuous for learning is but to repeat that his chief powers were moral not intellectual. Patience, endurance, tenacity, energy, and will — these, despite his ignorance, made him great. Cupidity and vanity, entailing boastfulness and craft, we have noted as his chief weaknesses; but as to cupidity the record is perhaps less vulnerable than it is at times represented. Throughout the years 1500 to 1504, the years preceding and including his fourth voyage, gold was to Columbus indeed a thing infinitely precious — precious in itself but far more so as the indispensable justification of his life and work. Then it is that we find him writing: "Gold is most excellent, gold is treasure, and he who possesses it does all he wishes to in this world, and succeeds in helping souls into Paradise."

Columbus was religious, formally and ceremoniously, albeit sincerely, religious. From an early date — in fact, while at Granada before his first voyage — he had embraced the idea of rescuing the Holy Sepulcher from the Infidel. To this end he was resolved, or so deemed himself, to devote his profits from the Indies. And withal he was eloquent. He waxed eloquent over the Holy Sepulcher; and when, after his third voyage, he was put upon waiting orders, alike to the impairment of his revenues and the wounding of his pride, he waxed eloquent over that injustice. "I have arrived at and am in such a condition," he writes in 1500, "that there is no person so vile but thinks he may insult me; he shall be reckoned in the world as valor itself who is courageous enough to consent to it. If I were to steal the Indies, or the land which lies toward them, of which I am now speaking, from the altar of St. Peter and give them to the Moors, they could not show greater enmity toward me in Spain. Who would believe such a thing where there was always so much magnanimity? . . . I undertook a fresh voyage to the new heaven and earth which up to that time had remained hidden; and if it is not held there in esteem like the other voyages to the Indies, that is no wonder because it came to be looked upon as my work."

His yet more famous letter, written in 1503 from

Jamaica, on his fourth voyage, is the cry of a Wolsey left naked to his enemies: "I was twenty-eight years old when I came into your Highnesses' service, and now I have not a hair upon me that is not gray; my body is infirm, and all that was left to me, as well as to my brothers, has been taken away and sold even to the frock that I wore, to my great dishonor. . . . I implore your Highnesses to forgive my complaints. I am indeed in as ruined a condition as I have related. Hitherto I have wept over others — may Heaven now have mercy upon me, and may the earth weep over me. . . . Weep for me, whoever has charity, truth, and justice!"

In the spirit of that charity, truth, and justice which Columbus here invokes, let it be said that, whatever his deflections from straightforwardness, he was not alone therein in his age or profession. Martin Behaim, Sebastian Cabot, and Amerigo Vespucci — not one of them as a navigator dealt honestly with his own age or with posterity. But, points of character aside, what in the case of the great Genoese most excites wonder, is not that he discovered America but that America should have remained to be discovered by him. The expedition of Telles, or that of Dulmo and Estreito

(Behaim), might well have reached the western continent. As early as 1500, indeed, Vicente Yañes Pinzón for Spain, and Pedralvarez Cabral for Portugal, touched the coast of South America.

Furthermore, as the region which was discovered by Columbus perpetuates, in the name Antilles, the mythical island of Antillia, so the region discovered by Pinzón and Cabral perpetuates in the name Brazil the mythical island of Brazil.

CHAPTER III

> . . . when with eagle eyes
> He stared at the Pacific — and all his men
> Looked at each other with a wild surmise —
> Silent, upon a peak in Darien.
>   KEATS: *On First Looking into Chapman's Homer*.

IN his Española letter of October, 1498, to the Spanish sovereigns, Columbus told them two things: first, that he had discovered the Earthly Paradise, which being on the top of the stem of the earth was "near heaven" and unattainable "save by God's permission"; and, second, that at Paria he had found pearls. The latter announcement was the moving one, and in 1499 two private expeditions set forth almost simultaneously to the Pearl Coast, one piloted by Juan de la Cosa but commanded by Alonso de Ojeda, a knight of truly Spanish audacity, companion of Columbus in 1493; and the other commanded by Pero Alonso Niño, one of Columbus's pilots in 1493 and 1498.

64

The voyage of Niño, so far as the gathering of riches was concerned, proved a success quite beyond anything achieved by Columbus, for it was rewarded by quantities of pearls. Ojeda was less successful in finding pearls, but he brought away some two hundred natives to be sold as slaves. In 1508 he was made Governor of the district of Urabá, which extended from the Darien (Atrato) River eastward to the Gulf of Venezuela and was called Castilla del Oro. West of Urabá, as far as Cape Gracias á Dios in Honduras, the coast, under the appellation of Veragua, was in 1508 assigned for government to Diego de Nicuesa, a rich and accomplished planter of Española.

The significance of Ojeda and Nicuesa, however, lies not so much in themselves as in their three associates — Vespucci, Balboa, and Pizarro; especially in Balboa, the true precursor of Cortés, with whom in a variety of respects he is not unworthy to be compared. As for Vespucci and Pizarro, the latter we shall meet presently, and the former need not long detain us. He was, be it said, an alert Florentine who as contractor's clerk had seen to the outfitting of the ships for the second voyage of Columbus, and who had accompanied Ojeda on his pearl-seeking voyage of 1499. He

5

had made three other transatlantic voyages, the third of which, by his literary handling of it in letters printed in Latin in 1504 and 1507 (the former under the title of *Mundus Novus*) had so established his fame that in 1507 Mundus Novus (South America) was beginning to be called Amerige — Americ's land or America.

But to revert to Balboa. Just as from the third voyage of Columbus, renowned for its pearls, there resulted the voyage of Ojeda, bringing to the mainland of the Indies Vespucci, so in 1500 there resulted the voyage of Rodrigo de Bastidas, bringing Vasco Núñez de Balboa. Of Balboa prior to this time we know only that he was a good "swordplayer," born in 1474 or 1475 in Estremadura. Luckless at sea with Bastidas, he had resorted to farming in Española, and when, in November, 1509, Ojeda and Nicuesa started for their provinces, he was restless to accompany one or other. Debt kept him back, but he was resourceful, and in September, 1510, when Ojeda's lieutenant, Martín Fernández de Enciso, prepared to follow his commander with supplies, Balboa, it is said, contrived to get himself smuggled on shipboard in a provision cask.

On the Venezuelan coast, near the present

Cartagena — for it was here that Enciso landed —
Balboa encountered Francisco Pizarro, a dutiful
soldier under Ojeda, with a boatload of Ojeda's
men. From him it was learned that Ojeda, having
lost De la Cosa in a fight, and being himself seri-
ously wounded, had founded the refuge of San
Sebastian, and then had departed for Española for
succor. His colonists, meantime, desperate with
hunger, were roaming hither and yon in quest of
food. All straightway betook themselves to San
Sebastian, but only to find it burned. The question then arose as to what should be done in circumstances so adverse.

In answer, up spoke Balboa. To the west of the
Gulf of Urabá was a region (Darien) abounding in
food; this he knew from having already visited
it under Bastidas. There, moreover, the Indians
used no poisoned arrows, missiles which had been
the undoing of the headlong Ojeda. Balboa was
of good stature, of knightly bearing, and of frank
address, and his words took effect. Ojeda's colony
transferred itself to Darien, where it founded Santa
María la Antigua del Darien, and — being thus
within the country which pertained to Nicuesa —
promptly on Balboa's suggestion deposed Enciso
and chose as alcaldes or judges Balboa and

Martín Zamudio; and, as regidor or alderman, a young nobleman, Juan de Valdivia.

Where, though, in the meantime was Nicuesa? Ojeda had reached New Andalusia with three hundred men and four small ships. Nicuesa had appeared off Castilla del Oro with nearly seven hundred men and five ships of large size, and was now sailing to and fro looking for Columbus's Veragua, the Golden Chersonese, but to no issue except the loss of ships and the drowning and starving of his men. Marooned at length upon desert sand, Nicuesa himself and sixty half-naked followers embraced despair. Some muttered, some raved, some in fierce irony laughed aloud. "A jest it was, ha! ha! a merry jest, to adventure life for gold, for lands, and to rule one's fellows!" Nicuesa was finally found and brought back to Darien by his lieutenant. But the colony, which was originally Ojeda's, distrusted Nicuesa and in March, 1511, putting him on board a leaky brigantine, dispatched him to Spain, and that was the last that they or any one heard of this overbearing commander.

At this time Diego Columbus, elder son of Christopher Columbus, presided over the Antilles as Governor and Admiral, with residence in Española.

On the continent of America (Tierra Firme), which now comprised Central America and Mundus Novus (South America), no one presided. Opportunity, therefore, called for a ruler in Tierra Firme and not in vain, for there was a man to respond — by name Vasco Núñez de Balboa. All he lacked was legal authorization. To obtain this, being so far from Spain, he must do mighty deeds, make himself potent and indispensable. And this he set himself to do. First, he deported Enciso to Spain, sending with him, to offset a possible misrepresentation of his action, the alcalde Zamudio. In the same ship, but commissioned to stop in Española and solicit the favor of Don Diego, he sent Valdivia. Don Diego proved malleable and soon appointed Balboa his lieutenant.

Thereupon Balboa shaped a career for conquest and discovery — a career in which two points that stand out are his recognition of Pizarro and his employment of blooded dogs. Francisco Pizarro was an Estremaduran, like Balboa, and of about the same age. He was ambitious, yet peculiar from the fact that in a period of restless competition he was content to bide, to serve, and to be ever dutiful. With regard to the dogs, they were no new thing with the Spaniard. Bartholomew Columbus had used them in Española, though not quite as Balboa was to use them in Darien. Their breed was of the best, and their fangs were deadly, but they were sagacious and under firm discipline.

Gold was Balboa's object but the prime immediate requisite was food. Careta, cacique of Cueva, a district to the west of Santa María, possessed both gold and food, and he possessed, furthermore, a daughter. Balboa attacked the village of Careta and carried the cacique and his attractive daughter prisoners to Santa María. Here, in turn, the captor himself was made captive, for he fell in love with the daughter, and formed with Careta an alliance against that cacique's enemy, Ponca.

To the west of Careta lay a rich and populous country of the Atlantic seaboard, ruled by a cacique, Comogre, who, to the amazement of the Spaniards, occupied a house constructed of posts and stone, with carved woodwork. An understanding with Comogre became practicable through the understanding with Careta, and momentous did it prove. It made of Balboa a discoverer, a world discoverer, the discoverer of the South Sea or Pacific Ocean — an achievement which, had it only come a little sooner, would

in all probability have brought with it the conquest of Peru.

Comogre had seven sons, one of whom, Panciaco,
was of marked intelligence. From him Balboa
learned of a cacique dwelling beyond a high sierra
on the Pacific side of the Isthmus of Darien and
possessed withal of much gold. This gold Balboa
resolved to see — the "baskets full," the "bags
full," the large "vessels" out of which the people
ate and drank. And he would see also the new
strange waters beyond the sierra, where, according
to report, were ships with sails and oars but little
less in size than those of the Spaniards themselves.
The difficulty confronting Balboa was that such
an adventure required many men, all seasoned
and well equipped — a thousand, Panciaco said, —
whereas the Spaniard had but a few hundred, and
these meager for lack of food.

So pressing, indeed, was the demand for food in
Darien that in January, 1512, Valdivia, back from
Española, was again sent forth, this time expressly
for provisions and to carry to Diego Columbus a
letter telling of the great southward-lying sea and
imploring the thousand men necessary for the
seizure of its golden littoral. Nor was this all, for
Balboa himself made an incursion into the country

of the cacique Dabaiba — a country not only by report an El Dorado but, what was more, one known to be stocked abundantly with grain.

Time sped and it now was October, 1512. Food had again run low, and men and equipment were as scarce as before. Valdivia had failed to return, nor had Española been otherwise heard from. But the determination of Balboa to establish himself in power by a successful South Sea venture remained unshaken. Commissioners were sent to Spain to unfold the situation to the King and to solicit aid of him directly. Hardly had they gone when two ships arrived from Diego Columbus bringing provisions and one hundred and fifty men. But they brought something even more important, and that was news — news from Spain. Zamudio wrote that, roused by Enciso's recital of the wrongs suffered by Nicuesa, King Ferdinand had ordered, first, that Balboa be brought home under criminal indictment; and, second, that Enciso himself be granted indemnification. Presumably Zamudio wrote also of a rumor that the King had in mind to appoint a Governor for Darien.

At any rate Balboa deemed it imperative to try to gain personally the royal ear, and on January

20, 1513, he addressed to Ferdinand his celebrated letter of exculpation, description, and appeal:

I desire to give an account to your most Royal Highness of the great secrets and marvelous riches of this land of which God has made your most Royal Highness the Lord, and me the discoverer before any other. . . . That which is to be found down this coast to the westward is the province called Careta, which is twenty leagues distant. . . . Further down the coast, at a distance of forty leagues from this city [Santa María], and twelve leagues inland, there is a cacique called Comogre. . . . In the mountains [to the southward] there are certain caciques who have great quantities of gold in their houses. It is said these caciques store their gold in barbacoas like maize, because it is so abundant that they do not care to keep it in baskets; that all the rivers of these mountains contain gold; and that they have very large lumps in great abundance. . . . I, Sire, have myself been very near these mountains, within a day's journey, but I did not reach them because I was unable to do so, owing to the want of men. . . . Beyond these mountains the country is very flat toward the south, and the Indians say that the other sea is at a distance of three days' journey. . . . They say that the people of the other coast are very good and well mannered; and I am told that the other sea is very good for canoe navigation, for that it is always smooth, and never rough like the sea on this side, according to the Indians. I believe that there are many islands in that sea. They say that there are many large pearls, and that the caciques have baskets of them. . . . It is a

most astonishing thing and without equal, that our Lord
has made you the lord of this land.

Then he asked for a thousand men from Española; for materials for the building of small ships
— "pitch, nails, ropes and sails"; for "master
shipwrights" and for arms — "200 crossbows with
very strong stays and fittings and with long ranges,
two dozen good handguns of light metal to weigh
not more than twenty-five to thirty pounds"; and
for "good powder."

None of Balboa's demands, however, were to be
granted.   Indeed, by the time his commissioners
reached Spain in May, 1513, it is probable that the
decision had been made to supersede him.   Of this,
as we have seen, he had received intimation, and,
with or without men and munitions, he must act.
Upon his action depended everything: his fame,
his fortune, and his life.

Balboa set forth on September 6, 1513, from
Careta's country (Caledonia Bay) directly southward across the Isthmus of Darien to the Gulf
of San Miguel.   With him he took one hundred
and ninety Spaniards.   He took, also, hundreds of
Indian slaves as attendants and burden bearers.
Careta's daughter was still his spouse, and through

this fortunate connection he obtained provisions and guides. The arms of his men were the usual swords, crossbows, and arquebuses; but more formidable than all other means of foray were the dogs, the bloodhounds.

The distance to be traversed was not great — about forty-five miles — but the obstacles were as formidable as the distance was trifling. A cacique named Quarequá proved the most redoubtable foe, and fell upon the Spaniards with a confident and yelling host. He was, however, quickly put to flight by the discharges from the crossbows and arquebuses; and after the fleeing men leaped the dogs. Then, drawing their swords, the Spaniards (according to Peter Martyr) made bloody havoc, "hewing from one an arme, from another a legge, from him a buttocke, from another a shoulder, and from some the necke from the bodie at one stroke."

The country at first was a succession of streams and swamps, screened by interlacing vines and creepers, the home of gorgeous flowers and brilliant birds, but no less the dwelling-place of countless chattering monkeys and inconvenient reptiles. Everywhere stretched forests of trees, stupendous, dark, and so festooned as to be almost impenetrable even to the ax. At length the journey was over. On the 25th of September, Balboa was at the base of an elevation which his guides told him looked upon the sea of the south — the Mar del Sur, as the Spaniards long henceforth were to call it. Some sixty-six or sixty-seven men only were equal to the ascent. With these Balboa clambered to a point near the summit. Bidding them pause, the ambitious explorer went "himselfe," says Peter Martyr, "alone to the toppe." Here he looked long and prayed; then he beckoned to his men, who gathered about him and stared at the Pacific.

Among the number thus silent upon a peak in Darien was Francisco Pizarro. To him the situation was a congenial one. Duty had been performed and there was no need for utterance. But what were his thoughts? In the "golden vessels" said to be used by Tubanamá, did he surmise anything of Peru? Quite likely not. Still, distant regions of a new civilization were now and again heard of in Darien. Once a refugee from "the great landes farre towarde the West" came upon a Spanish official reading, and, starting with surprise, exclaimed: "You, also, have books!"

But this by the way. Pizarro, the dutiful captain, was now straightway sent forward by Balboa

BALBOA TAKING POSSESSION OF THE PACIFIC OCEAN

Engraving in Herrera's *Historia General*

PONCE DE LEON IN FLORIDA

Engraving in Herrera's *Historia General.*

BALBOA TAKING POSSESSION OF THE PACIFIC OCEAN

Engraving in Herrera's Historia General.

PONCE DE LEON IN FLORIDA

Engraving in Herrera's Historia General.

Vasco Nuñez toma posesion de la Mar del Sur

Ju. Ponce pelea con is. de la Florida

Gravura Andersen–Lamb Co. N.Y.

to discover the shore of the sea they had gazed upon, and on September 29, 1513 — St. Michael's day — Balboa himself, with drawn sword and uplifted banner, advanced to meet the tide. They stood facing a gulf, and in honor of the day they named it San Miguel. And here there came to the Spaniards an unmistakable intimation of Peru. Tumaco, cacique of one of the gulf tribes, replying to questions by Balboa as to the extent of this new coast, told him that the mainland extended to the south without end, and that far in that direction dwelt a nation fabulously rich, who sailed the ocean in ships and used beasts of burden. To illustrate the beasts, he formed from clay the figure of the llama, which seemed a kind of camel. "This," says Herrera, the Spanish historian, "was the second intimation Vasco Núñez [and we may add Francisco Pizarro] had of Peru."

In 1513 Darien was still to explorers, as it had been to Columbus, the Malay Peninsula, the Golden Chersonese, the approach to India. "It is thought," notes the indefatigable Martyr, "that not far from the colony of San Miguel lies the country where the fruitfulnesse of spice beginneth." To dispel this illusion there was required the voyage of Magellan, a voyage not merely to America but through America and beyond it. Prior to the time of this voyage in 1519–1522, America was thought of only as a part of the continent of Asia. Magellan detached America and gave it an independent existence.[1]

But at the time of the discovery of the South Sea itself Columbus's idea of America as a land appurtenant and subsidiary to Asia prevailed, and had Balboa reached Peru or Mexico he would have believed himself in India. Even by Cortés, Mexico was thought to be the Golden Chersonese.

After discovering the Gulf of San Miguel and finding Isla Rica, rich in pearls, Balboa turned northward and reached Santa María on January 19, 1514. Here the whole people welcomed him and eagerly viewed his treasure. For once in the

[1] Nearly two years after the discovery of America it became necessary to adjust the claims of Spain and Portugal to territories in the West, and, as a result of negotiations, a line was fixed by the Treaty of Tordesillas, June 7, 1494, bisecting the earth at 370 leagues west of the Cape Verde Islands. To the east of this line, what might be found was to belong to Portugal; to the west of it, to Spain. It was the idea of Magellan, sailing in the service of Spain, as it had been that of Columbus, that the Spice Islands and China could be reached by way of the west; but it was not his idea that Asia had been found in America. He expected to pass through America by an interoceanic strait and to gain the Spice Islands somewhere in the South Sea beyond.

Indies, however, treasure to the Spaniards was a thing of secondary account. The new sea was what these men cared about. The Mar del Sur — what of it? From Darien Balboa dispatched Pedro de Arbolancha as a special messenger to Ferdinand with the great news. And, as typical of the new sea and of the auriferous realms whereto supposedly it was tributary, he entrusted to his messenger by way of gift for the King not merely gold but two hundred lustrous pearls, the fruit of the waters of this great southern sea.

But if tales of wealth in the West had given to Balboa his rise, similar tales were to contribute to his fall. A story gained currency that in Darien the natives were accustomed "to fish for gold with nets." The prospect of such fishing appealed with special force to an elderly gentleman of Segovia — Pedro Arias de Ávila; and, as Balboa was to be displaced, and Arias (or Pedrarias as he is known) had money and friends, he was made Governor with jurisdiction reaching from the Gulf of Maracaibo to Cape Gracias á Dios.

The expedition of Pedrarias set sail from San Lúcar on April 11, 1514. Prior to this time one of the greatest expeditions to leave Spain for the Indies had been the second commanded by

Columbus, which had sailed from Cadiz in 1493.   In
point of eminence, however, the names connected
with the expedition of Pedrarias outshone those of
its early predecessor in high degree.   There were,
for example, Gonzalo Fernández de Oviedo, who
together with Las Casas had beheld the triumph
of Columbus after his first voyage; Francisco Vásquez Coronado de Valdés, Quixotic and chivalric
seeker after the Seven Cities of Cibola; Hernando
de Soto, discoverer of the Mississippi; and Bernal
Díaz del Castillo, companion-to-be of Cortés and
rugged chronicler of his deeds.

Many adventurers, some two thousand men who
were anxious to go, had to be left behind for want
of room.   Those taken numbered about fifteen
hundred, and the show they made was brilliant
enough.   Largely they were young nobles and
gentlemen who had expected to follow Gonsalvo
de Córdoba to the Italian wars, and they came
wearing their silks and brocades and provided with
gleaming armor for which they had gone heavily
into debt.   "Upon the imagination of such,"
writes Washington Irving, "the very idea of
an unknown sea and splendid empire broke with
the vague wonders of an Arabian tale."   Finally,
Pedrarias brought with him his wife, the resolute

Isabel de Bobadilla, and a bishop for Darien —
the first prelate of Tierra Firme — Juan de Quevedo. Both the lady and the bishop, it is worthy
to be remarked, fell under the spell of the gallan-
try of Vasco Núñez de Balboa.

As for Pedrarias himself, he was skillful with
the lance and had fought against the Portuguese
and the Moors, but was now elderly and somewhat
infirm. In temper he was arbitrary and wily.
Sir Arthur Helps deems him "a suspicious, fiery,
arbitrary old man"; an epigrammatic American
thinks he had a "swarthy soul"; and even John
Fiske pronounces him "a green-eyed, pitiless,
perfidious old wretch." His first business was to
arrest Balboa and bring him to trial for misdeeds
against Enciso and Nicuesa; but the charges fell
flat, save that Enciso, who had been given office
under Pedrarias, was awarded civil damages for
loss of property.

Then for a period Balboa was ignored, and the
followers of Pedrarias, mad for gold, were let loose
upon the Isthmus. Between June 30, 1514, and
January, 1517, a dozen expeditions, sent ostensibly
to connect the Atlantic Ocean with the Pacific,
ravaged the country. The cruelties inflicted upon the natives were monstrous.   "Some," says

6

Oviedo, "were roasted, others were mangled by dogs, others were hanged." Driven to desperation, the Indians at length turned upon their persecutors. Spaniards when caught were not only slain but were tortured to death. Legs and arms were severed by sharp stones, or the captive was bound and gagged and molten gold was poured down his throat, the Indians meanwhile in mockery bidding the helpless Christians, "Eat, eat, and take your fill!"

On leaving his ships, Pedrarias had sought to impress the Darien settlers with his might and magnificence. But the silken and brocaded lords and gentlemen who so largely constituted his retinue had not turned out well. Disease and famine had fast laid hold upon them, forcing them to barter scarlet tunics for corn or to feed on herbage or to drop exhausted in the wilderness until "their souls deserted them" — full seven hundred of them.

Still these untoward circumstances, bad as they were, were not what exasperated Pedrarias most. At his side — inactive, but observing, cogitative, and critical — stood Balboa, whom nothing escaped. Writing to the King on October 16, 1515, Balboa, with a touch of the style of Mark Antony, describes the Governor as "an honorable man," but one who "takes little heed of the interest of your Majesty, and one in whom reigns all the envy and avarice in the world." Alluding to the cruelties to the Indians, he calls them "the greatest ever heard of in Arabian or Christian country," and says that whereas these Indians "formerly were as sheep, now they are as fierce as wolves."

Had Pedrarias been less unsuccessful in governing than he was, no single jurisdiction could have continued to hold both him and Vasco Núñez de Balboa. They were incompatible beings, of whom one must go down before the other. How true this was became apparent when, early in 1515, the full strength of Pedrarias's resentment was evoked through jealousy.

Balboa's messenger, Arbolancha, who had been sent to report to Ferdinand the discovery of the South Sea, had reached Spain but shortly after the departure of Pedrarias. With his gold, his pearls, and his magic tales of Balboa's preëmption of the realms of Ophir, Arbolancha quite won over Ferdinand, especially as Balboa had cost the Crown nothing, whereas Pedrarias had cost it much. Balboa was thereupon created Adelantado of the

South Sea and Captain-General of Cueva and Panamá under the nominal supervision of Pedrarias as Governor of Darien. The Governor well knew that an adelantadoship, though technically a lieutenancy, was in reality a provincial governorship — a kind of proconsulship — and something which, in the hands of a Balboa, might easily be transformed into a position of independent power.

To Pedrarias two courses lay open. One was to forestall the new Adelantado by going to the Pacific seaboard himself. The other was to institute against him further public proceedings during the pendency of which his commission might be withheld. Emphasizing the first course, Pedrarias sent Gaspar de Morales and Francisco Pizarro to the west shore of the Gulf of San Miguel to seize the Pearl Islands; and he sent yet farther west an expedition which reached the peninsula of Parita. He in person founded Aclá on the Atlantic coast near the site of the subsequent Caledonia Harbor, and, through Gaspar de Espinosa, alcalde mayor or chief judge of Darien, penetrated to the extreme west as far as the Gulf of Nicoya in the present Costa Rica.

The second course against Balboa, the withholding of his commission, proved wholly a failure, for the Bishop of Darien, to whom it was of necessity disclosed, denounced it roundly in public from the pulpit.

Events now moved apace. Balboa, after the interview of Arbolancha with Ferdinand, received a letter from the King, written in August, 1514, informing him that Pedrarias had been instructed to "treat him well." With this assurance Balboa had therefore resolved to make his adelantadoship a reality by exploring the coasts of the South Sea regardless of the Governor.

By secretly obtaining supplies from Cuba, Balboa nearly brought about his own downfall, but the situation was retrieved by Bishop Quevedo, who persuaded Pedrarias (very possibly Doña Isabel was here a factor) to become reconciled and give to the courtly Balboa his eldest daughter, Doña María, in betrothal. The arrangement, whatever may have been the motive of Pedrarias in countenancing it, in nowise changed his feeling toward Balboa — an instinctive jealousy and suspicion. To Balboa, on the contrary, the arrangement was not unpleasing. He still loved Careta's daughter; Doña María was at school in Spain; his marriage with her could be deferred. Pedrarias meanwhile could not well oppose the passage of the Adelantado, his prospective son-in-law, to the latter's province on the Pacific.

What Balboa needed was ships. These, to the number of four brigantines, he built from the forest on the northern side of the sierra below Aclá; and thousands of impressed Indians carried them in sections over the ridge to the waters of the river Balsas (Sabana?), which flowed into the Gulf of San Miguel. But the timbers proved rotten, and the work of shipbuilding had to be done all over again. Done, however, it finally was; and Balboa stood exultant on the beach of Isla Rica gazing seaward. The nights at this season were clear, we are told, and a certain great star rode in the heavens above. Now it seems that just after Balboa's discovery of the Pacific, a Venetian traveling astrologer who was in Santa María had pointed out to him the star, telling him that when it attained in the heavens a definite point he was to beware, as mortal peril faced him. The crisis safely passed, he would be Fortune's child — "the greatest lord and captain in all the Indies, and withal the richest." Turning to friends who were with him, Balboa on one occasion spoke of the star and ridiculed the astrologer. "Have I not," he said, "three hundred men and four ships and the countenance, officially, of Pedrarias!"

From time to time news had reached Darien that, as Balboa had been superseded by Pedrarias, so the latter was to be superseded by Lope de Sosa, acting Governor of the Canary Islands. Such news, now that Balboa was on working terms with Pedrarias, was not welcome to him, for a change in governors might cause him delay. So the Adelantado remarked to his notary that it would be well to send to Aclá to ascertain whether Lope de Sosa were yet arrived. If he were, then Balboa could not put to sea too soon. If he were not, some much needed iron and pitch might be obtained, and the preparations could be continued. Four men composed the party to go to Aclá: Andrés Garabito, Luis Botello, Fernando Múñoz, and Andrés de Valderrábano. They were to make their visit by night and to gather information from the servant who would be found in Balboa's house.

But the crisis foretold by the astrologer and registered by the star had come. Garabito under a dissembling exterior hated Balboa for having admonished him against attempted familiarities with Careta's daughter. He had even written to Pedrarias that Balboa cared naught for Doña

María, to whom he was betrothed, and meant at the earliest opportunity to renounce the Governor personally as well as politically. Furthermore, the remark of Balboa about a speedy putting to sea had been overheard by a sentry, who, mistaking it for treason, had so reported it to Garabito or Botello. Finally, the period within which the Adelantado was to be ready for sea, under agreement with the Governor, had been much exceeded and Pedrarias would not extend it; and when Balboa's chief financial backer, Fernando de Argüello, wrote advising a putting to sea at once, the letter was intercepted.

Garabito and Botello on their nocturnal visit to Aclá were both apprehended, and what they related to Pedrarias deeply implicated Balboa in disloyalty and intrigue. How the story roused Pedrarias, primitive Spaniard that he was, to a cold fury, distinctly appears in the counter measures which he took. To Balboa he penned a beguiling letter, inviting him to come to Aclá. To Francisco Pizarro — the model subordinate, the ever-dutiful one — he at the same time gave orders to gather a force, meet Balboa, and arrest him. The Adelantado came. Warnings he received, but he disregarded them. Before he had crossed

the sierra he was met by Pizarro's force. The
leader himself stepped forward and made the
arrest. "It is not thus," said Balboa, smiling
sadly, "that you were wont to come forth to receive me, Francisco Pizarro."

Balboa's trial was conducted by the alcalde
mayor or chief judge, Gaspar de Espinosa, and
the Adelantado's entire record, from the days of
Encisu and Nicuesa, was admitted against him.
Even so he would have been allowed an appeal to
the Crown, had it not been for the Governor, who
would not assent to it.

At Santa María, in the plaza, a scaffold and
block were prepared, and early in the morning of
a day in January, 1519, Balboa was led forth in
chains. Before him walked the town crier ex-
claiming: "Behold the traitor and usurper!" "'Tis
false!" retorted Balboa, "never have I been dis-
loyal!" With this, he mounted the scaffold and
received the sacrament. His head was then cut
off upon a hatchment cloth and stuck upon a
pole. The same day, until past nightfall, were
beheaded in ghastly succession Valderrábano, Botello, Múñoz, and Argüello. Pedrarias, it is said,
witnessed the executions from behind the shelter
of a lattice; while as for Garabito, he reaped a

not uncommon reward of treachery in the salvation of his own life.

Thus the third voyage of Columbus, the voyage for pearls, brought about, as a first great result, the occupation of that part of the mainland of America now known as the Isthmus of Panamá and the discovery of the Pacific Ocean. As its second great result, it brought about, though less directly, the occupation of Mexico, a tale which remains to be told.

CHAPTER IV

CORTÉS AND MEXICO

Where dwell the gods?
Where dwell the gods?
Oh dwell they in the sky?

.   .   .   .

The gods are always nigh.

RAYMOND: *The Aztec God.*

BUT what of the young nobleman — Valdivia? "O
you wretched men of Darien," exclaims Peter
Martyr, "tarry for Valdivia whom you sent to
provide to helpe your necessities? Provide for
yourselves rather, and trust not to them whose
fortune yee know not."

Juan de Valdivia, it will be remembered, had in
January, 1512, set out from Santa María of Darien
for Española to solicit of Don Diego Columbus a
supply of food. His return, long looked for, never
came. His ship was wrecked off Jamaica, and he
was carried in an open boat with a few followers
to the coast of Yucatán. Here he was seized by

the local cacique and with three others was sacrificed to the gods, his heart being torn out and his flesh eaten. Some of the company were kept prisoners. One by one they died till two only were left — Gonzalo Guerrero, a seaman, and Gerónimo de Aguilar, a friar — both of whom some eight years later were found, as will be seen, by Cortés.

Columbus never reached Yucatán, but on his first voyage he heard of the culture of a people called the Mayas, who wore clothes and dwelt on a mainland ten days' journey in a canoe from Española; and on his fourth voyage he came, on July 30, 1502, into actual touch with this civilization, near the island of Guanaja, off the coast of Honduras. Here he encountered a monster canoe provided with an awning and laden with merchandise; a canoe bearing a cacique clad in loin cloth and mantle; one, furthermore, which was being propelled by a band of twenty-five Indians "well clothed." Nor was Columbus's acquaintance with the Maya culture limited to the sight of the canoe. Near Cariari (Nicaragua) he personally visited a mountain tomb, "as large as a house and elaborately sculptured," where there stood, or crouched, as though peering within, the corpse of a Maya Indian. He saw also, he tells us, "some large sheets of cotton cloth elaborately and cleverly worked, and other sheets [Maya manuscripts?] very delicately painted."

As compared with the Nahuas of Mexico (pre-Aztec as well as Aztec), the Mayas of Yucatán were an ancient, a peaceful, and a polished race; and, like all races that have advanced as far as barbarism, they were emphatically religious. Their most characteristic deity, perhaps, was Itzamna, god of the East or rising sun, inventor of letters. But there was another sun deity, Kukulcan, the most active and immanent of the Maya gods. He was patron of arts and crafts, inculcator of peace, and withal deprecator of human sacrifices — a god of order who, having founded cities, had departed into the sunrise, whence he had promised to return at a future time. War gods there were in the Maya pantheon, but war and religion, despite some human sacrifices, were not the intimate blend that they were in Mexico.

If the death of Valdivia and his three fellow unfortunates upon a heathen altar may be regarded as demanding of Heaven to be avenged, vengeance nevertheless was somewhat delayed. Valdivia died in 1512. Up to that time but little had been done to subdue and occupy the Antilles

outside of Española. In 1509 Diego Columbus had
sent a Governor to Jamaica, and in 1511 he had
made Diego Velásquez Governor of Cuba — a land
which Christopher Columbus had never recognized
as insular, but which had been officially demon-
strated so to be by a voyage of circumnavigation
effected by Sebastián de Ocampo in 1508. Velásquez was jocose and affable but at the same time
acquisitive and envious. To Cuba he took with
him, or soon summoned to follow him, Francisco
Hernández de Córdoba, Juan de Grijalva, Bartolomé de las Casas, Pánfilo de Narváez, and
Hernan Cortés. Narváez did the work of pacifica-
tion, while Velásquez founded Trinidad, Puerto
del Príncipe, Matanzas, Santo Espíritu, San Salvador, Habana, and Santiago.

In 1516, because of the continued famine in
Darien, Governor Pedrarias gave leave to his silken
host, as many as wished, to go to Cuba, where
provisions were not lacking. And one hundred
and ten went. Velásquez met them cordially and
promised them land if they would wait for vacan-
cies, but they were tired of a passive rôle and
craved activity. Slave catching, though contrary
to law, was at this time practised in the island,
and it no doubt was with the profits from such an

enterprise in view that the Darien arrivals made ready an expedition which would serve as an outlet for their energies. They chartered two vessels, Velásquez, it is said, contributing a third, and on February 8, 1517, with Hernández de Córdoba, now a rich planter of Santo Espíritu, as captain, unfurled their sails from San Cristóbal, the old Habana.

Whither should they fare? Their chief pilot counseled adventuring straight into the west, into the region of the people who "wore clothes." The squadron, about the 1st or 2d of March, reached the island of Las Mugeres (Island of Women), and on the 4th landed at Point Catoche, the extreme northeasterly limit of Yucatán. Their next landing was at Champotón, in Campeche, whence they tediously worked their way back to San Cristóbal by way of the peninsula of Florida. On this expedition the Spaniards were roughly handled by the natives. Both Córdoba and Bernal Díaz were wounded, the former so severely that soon after reaching Cuba he died. But the invaders succeeded in bringing away two youths whom they named, respectively, Melchor and Julian, and to whom they taught Spanish, that they might serve as interpreters.

Foiled as to slave catching but curious regarding Yucatán, the Cuban settlers by 1518 were ready for a second adventure into the west, and this time it was Velásquez who took the lead. He managed to add two vessels to two others left from the expedition of Córdoba, enlisted some two hundred and fifty men, and appointed Juan de Grijalva commander-in-chief. Sail was made from Santiago de Cuba on the 8th of April, with Alaminos once more as chief pilot, and on the 3d of May the fleet gained, to the southward of Point Catoche, a large island called Cozumel (Island of Swallows). By the last of the month the expedition had passed Lake Terminos, and by the 18th of June various rivers of Tabasco, such as Río de Grijalva and Río de Banderas, and various islands off Mexico, including San Juan de Ulúa and Isla de Sacrificios. They made a landing where now stands the city of Vera Cruz.

Grijalva, under the orders given him, might trade in any regions discovered, but he might not colonize, and, as the country everywhere by its aspect invited to colonization, Alvarado on the 24th of June was permitted to sail for Cuba to carry back the sick, report progress, and, if possible, obtain permission to form settlements.

Meanwhile Grijalva followed the Mexican coast as far north as Cape Rojo, whence, returning to Yucatán, he sailed for Cuba, reaching Matanzas about the 1st of November.

On both the Córdoba and Grijalva expeditions the Spaniards were impressed by divers things, but more than with anything else by the scenery, the sacrificial mounds, and the stone temples. On every island, and dotting the coast of the mainland, were to be seen mounds pyramidal in form, ascended by stone steps, and surmounted by temple towers of squat masonry. The towers gleamed white, and over them floated the smoke of incense and of sacrifice. At Campeche, Córdoba saw many temples or "prayer-places" wetted within with fresh blood. From each there swarmed angrily forth half a score of priests, armed with braziers, and clad in white mantles down which fell their hair, long, black, and disheveled — so matted and clotted with blood, from their own ears lacerated in penance, that one strand could not be separated from another. Indeed the farther to the west the Spaniards fared — the closer their approach, that is to say, to the Nahua tribes of Mexico as distinguished from the Maya of Yucatán — the more the evidences of human sacrifices multiplied.

7

"Why," asked Grijalva of a Tabasco Indian, "this ripping open of human bodies and offering of bloody hearts to hungry gods?" "Because," was the reply, "the people of Ulúa [by which was meant Mexico] will have it so."

When, in November, 1518, Grijalva reached Cuba — then called Isla Fernandina — he found himself most undeservedly out of favor. He was young, handsome, and chivalric, but above all conscientious, so conscientious that Las Casas tells us he would have made a good monk. Having been ordered not to plant colonies, he had obeyed. But obedience proved to be his undoing, for, angered by it, his subordinates, particularly Alvarado, whom he had reproved, had misrepresented him to Velásquez, and already that grasping ruler had decided upon a new voyage in which Grijalva was not to share.

For this new voyage Velásquez sought a commander of quite supermundane qualities — one astute and valiant enough to achieve rare deeds and at the same time subservient enough to give all the honors and emoluments to Velásquez. The Governor, profiting by Grijalva's labors, had already on the 13th of November secured for himself the adelantadoship of all that "he had discovered" in the West or "might thereafter discover" there, and his solicitude to make just the right choice of a commander was intense. Then, as not seldom in human affairs, stepped in Fate — ironical, mocking Fate. To Diego Velásquez, tremulous with apprehension lest he choose wrongly for himself, Fate dictated the selection of Hernan Cortés!

It has been said that the rise of Cortés was due to the third voyage of Columbus; and the statement is true in that his rise was part of the movement following upon Columbus's pearl discoveries — a movement which, through Nicuesa and Ojeda, begat Balboa; and, through Balboa, begat Pedrarias; and, through Pedrarias, those activities in Cuba which resulted in the expeditions of Córdoba and Grijalva. Apropos of Columbus, in this connection, regret at times has found voice that it was not he who conquered Mexico rather than Cortés. There, it is said, he would have found fulfillment of his dream of gold, if not of spicery, in measure far more complete than in Asia and India, for in the fifteenth century the Cathay of Marco Polo, as also Polo's Cipangu, were vanished things. But to each his task. The Mexican conquest called for traits at least one of which, ruthlessness, Columbus did not possess. It called, that is to say, for the traits which were peculiarly Spanish, and it called for all of them — for ruthlessness, for pride, for devoutness, and for romanticism. These traits, combined and co-ordinated in a unique manner, belonged to Cortés.

Hernan Cortés was born in Medellin, in Estremadura, in 1485. His parents were — as who in those days in Spain was not? — of noble descent though poor. As he was delicate in health, he was destined for the law. At fourteen he entered the University of Salamanca, where he remained two years, acquiring a smattering of Latin and some ease in rhetoric. On leaving the university he looked about him. He might join the banner of the Great Captain, Córdoba, as had been the frustrated purpose of so many of the followers of Pedrarias, or he might go to the Indies. The Indies were his choice, and thither in 1504 he took passage.

This was the period just subsequent to the coming of Nicolás de Ovando to Española as Governor, and Cortés after some hesitation was induced by Ovando to become a planter. In 1510 he would have joined Nicuesa on his Veragua

HERNANDO CORTÉS

Painting by an unknown artist. In the Hospital de Jesus, City of Mexico. This portrait is said to have been presented to the Hospital by Cortés himself.

(Castilla del Oro) expedition, but was prevented
by an abscess under the right knee. In 1511 Diego
Velásquez, who admired his intelligence, took him
to Cuba as business adviser or private secretary.
Cortés was young and famed for his amorous
gallantries. According to reports not altogether
illuminating, his "affairs" in Cuba involved him
in discord with Velásquez. Catalina Suárez was
the name of one of his inamoratas, and her he
married. By 1518 Velásquez, despite differences,
had appointed him alcalde at Santiago de Cuba.
Cortés was now thirty-three. He was of medium
stature, compact and muscular, and had dark eyes,
good features, a short beard, and legs a trifle
bowed. Outwardly he was frank and vivacious,
but inwardly he was calculating and self-contained.

Since 1516 in Española, Diego Columbus, as
Admiral and Governor, had been under the super-
visory authority of three monks, known as the
Jeronimite Fathers, who had been sent to the
Indies at the instance of Las Casas to temper
somewhat with mercy the dealings of Spaniards
with the natives, and it was necessary to obtain
from them sanction for enterprises such as that
for which Velásquez had selected Cortés. Velásquez obtained the requisite sanction and, on the

23d of October, before Grijalva's own return from the west, he issued instructions authorizing (as in Grijalva's case) exploration but not colonization.

Cortés was now energy itself. He mortgaged his estate; he secured a large contribution from Velásquez; he stuck a plume in his bonnet; he hoisted a banner; he issued proclamations. By these means and by enacting throughout a jovial rôle, he gathered out of Cuba and Jamaica eleven vessels, 508 soldiers, and 109 seamen by February 10, 1519. But there were difficulties, and the gravest of these was a distrust of Cortés which was more and more perceptibly defining itself in the mind of the Governor.

Like the chorus in the drama of antiquity, the fool or jester of early modern drama performed a work of prognosis. He forecast the issue. Such a fool Diego Columbus had about him, officially, in the person of a sharp-witted dwarf named Francisquillo. This oracle, unlike the fool in *Lear*, did not say openly to his master: "Thou had'st little wit in thy bald crown when thou gav'st thy golden one away," but he said what was equivalent to it. To Velásquez — as one day, along with Cortés, he surveyed the harbor of Santiago alive with the preparation of Cortés's fleet — Francisquillo, who was capering about, exclaimed: "Have a care, Diego, Diego, lest this Estremaduran captain of yours make off with the fleet!" Herein, it is said, the distrust on the part of Velásquez took its rise.

Cortés did not slink from Santiago with his ships in the night. He left openly in the daytime after embracing the Governor, but he was nevertheless closely watched. Indeed Velásquez's distrust of him continued to grow, for he made frantic efforts to supersede him at Trinidad and to stop him and apprehend him at San Cristóbal.

In his train Cortés took a notable band of Spanish gentlemen — ten stanch captains each in command of a company, with himself in command of the eleventh. The arms carried were thirty-two crossbows, thirteen firelocks, and an outfit of swords and spears, the whole reënforced by artillery in the form of ten bronzed guns — breech-loaders! — and four falconets. But above and beyond all else were sixteen noble horses, about which more anon. The general rendezvous was Cape San Antonio, the most westerly point of Cuba, whence on the 18th of February the expedition — all save Pedro de Alvarado's ship, which was driven aside by tempest — set its prows for Cozumel.

At this time there was no knowledge in the Indies of the fate of the Valdivia party, but on the Córdoba expedition Indians of Campeche had saluted the Spaniards with the word "Castilan," and this was deemed significant. At any rate after much inquiry on the Yucatán coast and much dispatching of messengers inland, Aguilar appeared, though Guerrero did not. Provided thus with a reliable interpreter — for Melchor and Julian had proved wanting and Aguilar was willing — Cortés early in March set sail with his fleet for the country of the cacique Tabasco.

The halting point of the Spaniards was an island in the Tabasco or Grijalva River, but when they sought to establish themselves on the mainland, christened by Cortés "New Spain," they were vigorously withstood. A fight took place on the 25th of March, and fortune was turned in favor of the Spaniards and against overwhelming bodies of Indians by the artillery and the horses.

In Darien, where the natives were lower in the scale of barbarism than in Yucatán and Mexico, Balboa had already won triumphs by the aid of powerful dogs. But to the east of the Gulf of Urabá, that region of the poisoned arrow, dogs had not been found effective; and in Yucatán

and Mexico — where the missiles most in use were
darts, javelins, slingstones, and the obsidian-
edged sword-club or *macuahuitl* — dogs, save for
hunting purposes, were eschewed. What in Darien
was accomplished by the dog was accomplished in
the region farther west by the horse.

At Tabasco, or rather on the plain of Ceutla
near by, the horses, supported by the cannon,
therefore won the day. The Indians, who
"covered the whole plain," who "wore great
feather crests" and "quilted cotton armor," who
carried "drums and trumpets" and rained upon
their foe arrows, javelins, and stones, were finally
hemmed in between the Spanish guns, which
ploughed through their masses, and the Spanish
horse, who under Cortés himself speared them
down, and so were brought to a stand. In the eyes
of the terrorized barbarians the guns with their
thunder and lightning were a marvel; but the
horsemen were a greater marvel still, for they were
each a living monster, horse and rider, in the words
of Bernal Díaz, "being all one animal."

It was at the close of this battle that the Tabas-
cans, suing for peace, brought to Cortés twenty
young women, among them Doña Marina, as she
came to be known — "a truly great chieftaness,

a daughter of caciques and a mistress of vassals."
Marina was Aztec, but as a little girl had been
given by her mother to the Indians of Tabasco in
order to make way for the succession of a half-
brother to the headship of her tribe. Cortés at
first did not bestow upon her especial notice,
merely assigning her to "a distinguished gentleman." What made her fortune was her knowledge
of both Nahua and Maya speech, combined with
her intelligence. The rescued Aguilar, who spoke
the Maya of Yucatán and Tabasco, readily understood the Maya of Tabasco as spoken by Marina.
So, as it proved, the chain of tongues indispensable
to Cortés was complete — Marina translating Aztec Nahua into Tabascan Maya, which Aguilar in
turn put into Castilian Spanish.

Cortés, who no less than Columbus was devout,
spent Palm Sunday of the year 1519 at Tabasco,
where a religious procession was held and mass
was sung, and where the Indians were stoutly
exhorted to give up their bloody sacrifices and
idols. The fleet then set sail and by Holy Thurs-
day was at the island of San Juan de Ulúa. Here
the Spaniards first came to a definite knowledge of
the existence and importance of Montezuma. It

is true that at Tabasco Grijalva had heard of a Culúa, or Ulúa, "where there was plenty of gold"; but, in the words of the chronicler, "we did not know what this Culúa could be."

At San Juan de Ulúa the fleet of Cortés lay at anchor, its fiery purpose clothed, as some one has said, in dissembling white. Hardly had it assumed its position when from two large canoes there ascended to the deck of the flagship a group of Indians. Asking for the Tlatoan, or Chief, they did him reverence, but beyond this they were unable to make themselves understood. Thereupon Marina, who with other slave girls was standing by, said to Aguilar that the Indians were Mexicans sent by the cacique Cuitlalpitoc, a servant of Montezuma, and that he wished to know whence the strangers had come and why. So was begun a series of interchanges between Cortés and the overlord of Culúa or Mexico — interchanges conducted on the part of the one with veiled though ever mounting audacity, and on the part of the other with veiled though ever deepening apprehension.

For more than a fortnight Cortés encouraged the coming of embassies — "for trade." First came Cuitlalpitoc accompanied by his superior,

Teuhtlilli; and with them they brought cotton fabrics done in brilliant feather designs — ten bales of them — as also articles of wrought gold set with rare stones. In return Cortés gave a carved and inlaid armchair, some engraved stones, a crimson cap, beads, and a gilt helmet which Teuhtlilli had wondered at and was told to bring back filled with gold dust. The Spaniard asked also for a time and place to be fixed at which he might meet Montezuma.

Then, in due season, came a second embassy, one headed by a cacique named Quintalbor, who in looks resembled Cortés. With Quintalbor came Teuhtlilli; and this time, besides cotton fabrics embroidered in feathers and gold, there were brought large plumes of bright colors spangled with gold and pearls; great feather fans; rods of gold like a magistrate's staff; collars and necklaces with pendant golden bells; head-dresses of green quetzal feathers and gold, or of feathers and silver; miniature golden fish; alligators, ducks, monkeys, pumas, and jaguars; a graceful bow with twelve sharp arrows — all these things, to say naught of Nahua books executed in picture-writing upon cotton or bark. Nor yet were these things all, for, dominating the entire collection, were a wheel of gold as large as a cart-wheel, a wheel of silver equally large (the twain worth in American money of today some $290,000), and the helmet at which Teuhtlilli had wondered filled with grains of gold fresh from the placers.

The object of this second embassy was clearly to bribe Cortés into leaving the country, for, to his wish again earnestly expressed to visit Montezuma many objections were courteously interposed. The refusal indeed was soon made pointed and explicit, for Teuhtlilli, having gone through the form of carrying to his lord the Spanish leader's reiterated request, came back after ten days bearing a quantity of robes, feathers, and gems as a gift to be carried by Cortés personally to his own over-lord, the Spanish King.

Having thus "felt out" Montezuma and his magnificence, Cortés saw his goal before him. But could he reach it? Reach it he must if he would escape outlawry. Already he had broken with Velásquez, for at Tabasco he had taken possession in the name of the King alone. His position was like that of Balboa after he had deported Enciso and had heard of the golden-shored Pacific. He must seize his opportunity. He must do or die.

As a first step Cortés resolved upon a new basis for his expedition. The soldiers must become a Spanish colony looking immediately to the King. Over this colony he himself must be chosen Captain-General and Justicia Mayor. As such he could found a settlement, taking care by destroying his fleet to remove from his followers all temptation to resume relations with Cuba and Velásquez. Even so, however, the situation for Cortés was fraught with difficulty. Assuming the successful establishment of direct relations with Charles V, successor to Ferdinand on the Spanish throne, how about the Indians? What would be their attitude toward the appropriation of Montezuma's wealth by the arrogant white strangers — the white strangers from out the sunrise? But just here a stroke of fortune!

Across the sand dunes above the San Juan de Ulúa anchorage, came one day, soon after the departure of the last of the embassies from Montezuma, five Indians. They were not Aztec, but two of their number spoke Nahua, and by aid of Marina and Aguilar it was quickly learned that they were Totonacs, subject to Montezuma and hating him with a deadly fear. Their principal settlement, Cempoalla, was a short distance inland to the

north, and here, eager for a conference with the
white chieftain, waited their cacique. Into the
hands of Cortés was given a possible solution of his
difficulty, and he was not slow to perceive it.

Cortés approached Cempoalla overland with
four hundred men and two light guns; while the
fleet ascended the coast some ten leagues to a
harbor called Bernal, discovered by Francisco de
Montejo. At the anchorage opposite San Juan de
Ulúa — the present Vera Cruz — it was not only
hot and damp, but according to Bernal Díaz "there
were always there many mosquitoes, both long-
legged ones and small ones."   The way to Cempoalla wound through tropical forest filled with
birds of startling plumage and dominated throughout by the snow-crowned peak of Orizaba, "Star
Mountain," gleaming in majesty to the south and
west. As for the settlement itself, it was the first
great town, the product of barbarism, which the
Spaniards had seen. From out a plaza rose
towered temples on pyramidal foundations; while
the sides of the square were formed by terrace-
roofed buildings of stone and adobe, the whole
brilliant with white stucco.

Cempoalla was dazzling, but no less was it
beautiful. Not only did it shine like silver, of

which some of the Spaniards at first thought it to
be constructed, but its houses were embowered in
green, and against this green and the white walls
beneath glowed the massed colors of tropical
flowers. Roses in particular abounded. As the
Spaniards entered and marched along, they were
met by deputations which showered roses upon the
horsemen. To Cortés some handed bouquets,
while others flung rose garlands about his neck or
placed wreaths on his helmet. The foot-soldiers,
too, were remembered, for to them were given
pineapples, cherries, juicy *zapotes*, and aromatic
anonas. The palace or official abode of the cacique was at length reached, and, though that per-
sonage was very sedate, he was so corpulent and
shook so when he walked that the Spaniards could
not be restrained from laughing at him.

Hardly had Cortés arrived in the Cempoallan
district when proof of the dread which the overlord
of Ulúa or Mexico inspired was dramatically revealed. Five of Montezuma's tribute men appeared. Haughty and insolent was their mien, and
upon them the Cempoallans attended like slaves.
"Their shining hair," says Bernal Díaz, "was
gathered up as though tied on their heads, and each
one was smelling the roses that he carried, and

each had a crooked staff in his hand." The meaning of the visit was that Montezuma resented the fact that Cempoalla was entertaining the white strangers, especially as by the last embassy sent to Cortés it had been made plain that their presence in Mexico was no longer desired. Explation, therefore, was demanded, and of the Cempoallan youth, men and maids, twenty must accompany the tribute men to Ulúa and yield their hearts upon the altar.

Cortés's purpose in Cempoalla was to cement an alliance with the Totonacs, yet to avoid as long as possible a break with the lord of Ulúa. He secretly ordered the Cempoallans to throw Montezuma's envoys into prison and to withhold tribute. At the same time he ingratiated himself with Montezuma by covertly liberating the prisoners and sending them to their lord with the tale of their deliverance at his hands. Montezuma therefore reopened relations with the Spanish leader by sending a further embassy bearing presents. Upon this delegation Cortés wrought with great effect by resorting to his never failing dependence — the horse. Verily, to the Mexicans, the neck of the horse was "clothed with thunder"; "the glory of his nostrils was terrible"; "he swallowed

8

the ground with fierceness and rage, and said among the trumpets 'ha! ha!'"

Having concluded an alliance with the Totonacs, Cortés founded in June, 1519, in Bernal Harbor his projected settlement, the town of Villa Rica de la Vera Cruz; and in July he sent to the King letters explanatory of the proceeding. Just prior to this, in renewed fury of missionary zeal — a fury which Father Olmedo, priest to the army, did his best somewhat to restrain — he had thrown down the idols at Cempoalla and cleansed the temples of blood. His next acts were to scuttle and sink his ships; to lash, mutilate, or hang, various Velásquez conspirators; and to frighten away an expedition sent out by the Governor of Jamaica. There now remained, as the one sole objective of the Spaniards in Mexico, Montezuma and his gold.

Montezuma is lord of many kings; his equal is not known in all the world; in his house many lords serve barefooted with eyes cast down to the ground; he has thirty thousand vassals in his empire each of whom has one hundred thousand fighting men; each year twenty thousand persons are regularly sacrificed in his dominions — some years fifty thousand. Montezuma dwells in the most beautiful, the largest, and the strongest city in the world — a city built in the water, possessing a noble palace and plaza, one the center of an immense

traffic. Hither flock princes from all the earth bringing
incalculable riches. No lord however great is there who
does not pay tribute, and no one so poor is there who
does not give at least the blood of his arm. The cost of
all is enormous, for, besides his household, Montezuma
is constantly waging war and maintaining vast armies.

These words of the cacique Olintetl echoed in the
ears of Cortés as, on August 31, 1519, he departed
from the friendly Totonac country on his way to
pay that visit to Montezuma which had been so
persistently declined. Had it been Columbus,
what more of confirmation would he have required
that he was about to behold the city and court of
the Great Kaan? As it was, even the practical-
minded Cortés felt himself impelled to write:
"According to our judgment, it is credible that
there is everything in this country which existed
in that from which Solomon is said to have brought
the gold for the Temple."

Mexico-Tenochtitlan, Abode of the War God,
the "Place of the Stone and Prickly Pear," seat of
the power of Montezuma, whereof the Spaniards
had heard under the name Ulúa, was a wonderful
place to the Spaniard, but he failed to understand
its real significance. What the Spaniard found in

Mexico, as he believed, was merely a "feudal monarchy" under a "king," supported by a "nobility" occupying "palaces" in a picturesque "city" full of "mosques." In point of fact Cortés unwittingly was looking across an abyss of perhaps ten thousand years — actually seeing the dead past live again. "To say," remarks John Fiske, "that it was like stepping back across the centuries to visit the Nineveh of Sennacherib or hundred-gated Thebes is but inadequately to depict the situation, for it was a longer step than that." Yes, immeasurably longer, for it was a step from civilization quite to mid-barbarism.

What it really was that Tenochtitlan disclosed to the Spaniards may perhaps be best conceived by the aid of a survey from the summit of one of the so-called mosques.

The Central Valley of Mexico is a plateau some 7400 feet above sea-level, about 60 miles long by 40 broad, and surrounded by mountains. Here the waters, collected by drainage as in a basin, spread themselves out in three shallow lakes or lagoons — of which Chalco and Xochimilico are fresh, and Tezcoco is salt — covering in all perhaps 442 square miles. Near the western side of Lake Tezcoco are two marsh islands, and over them

extends the community of Mexico-Tenochtitlan with its adjunct Tlatelolco. This community, which is not at all a "city" or municipality, is of about one-fourth the extent of the Mexico City of the present day, and harbors at this early time a population of perhaps 70,000 souls. Connection with the mainland is maintained by three long causeways — one to the north, one to the west, and one to the south — each 20 or 25 foot broad, and of a cement construction which is hard and smooth. These causeways, provided as they are with sluice gates, serve also as dikes for regulating the flow and depth of the water to the west of the islands, where it discharges from Chalco and Xochimilico, which are at a higher elevation than Tezcoco. For similar control to the eastward of the islands, a long dike exists. Besides the three main causeways there are certain tributary ones and a double aqueduct of concrete bringing water from the mainland hill of Chapultepec.

Turning now our gaze more directly beneath, we perceive first that the center of the main community, Tenochtitlan, is marked by a great square 900 by 1050 feet, facing the cardinal points and surrounded by a stone wall eight or nine feet high, embellished with carved stone serpents. In this

wall, on each side of the square, there is a gate, and
each gate is approached from without by a broad
avenue, those leading to the north, south, and west
gates being prolongations of the causeways. By
the square and avenues the main community is
divided into four quarters, the adjunct Tlatelolco
constituting a fifth division; and each quarter is
intersected by canals spanned by bridges. The
great square in Tenochtitlan forms the place of
trade and concourse, and in Tlatelolco a like square
subserves the same end.

So far as buildings are concerned, they are of
four principal sorts: first, huge communal dwellings;
next, official edifices or *tecpans;* then armories or
"houses of darts," as they are called; and, lastly, temple structures comprehending educational
houses and quarters for priests. The material of
all is a reddish stone, for the most part whitened
to brilliance by stucco; and the foundations as a
rule are pyramidal in shape. The great square is
filled with temples — twenty, at least, without
counting the chief temple; and Tlatelolco also
has its temples, a chief and lesser ones.

If the hour of observation from our mosque be
sunset, the picture will be charming. In the "pale
blue water sheet of Tezcoco" will be reflected not

alone the white buildings of Mexico-Tenochtitlan but those of other similar communities on the shores, the whole relieved against a dark blue sierra crowned by the peaks, gigantic and roseate, of Yztaccihuatl, "White Woman," and Popocatepetl, "Smoking Mountain." On the other hand, if we look at night, charm will be replaced by an aspect weirdly sinister. Spectral barks or canoes — fifty thousand of them, it is said — will be darting athwart the lake and through the brazier-lighted canals; while aloft the darkness will everywhere be pierced by temple flames. A modern smelting works, somewhat softened, might suggest the effect.

Open daylight, however, will best reveal Mexico-Tenochtitlan to the high-placed observer. By it the communal dwellings will be seen to be of wide extent, but of only one or at most two stories — in the latter case receding or terraced — and provided with low parapets. The principal *tec-pans*, of which there are two — one being in Tlatelolco — are surmounted by observation towers, and the pyramids of the temples are bulky structures of smooth stone, dented on one or more sides by steps and culminating in wooden oratories.

Terrible, indeed, is the religion of the Aztec Nahua! Its leading deity is Huitzilopochtli, god of war, and to him chiefly is consecrated the greatest pyramid of all. It stands in the broad square of Tenochtitlan; it is three hundred feet wide on each side at the base, and with its oratories it rises to a height of one hundred and fifty feet. Here, under one's very nostrils, as one gazes, reeks the blood of human sacrifices — blood-offerings performed by filthy priests, who, in the curt phrase of Bernal Díaz, "stink like sulphur and have another bad smell like carrion."

A second great deity shares with the war god his ensanguined abode — Tezcatlipoca, god-of-the-breath-of-life, the racial god of the Nahua. Near by are the temples of two other important gods: Tlaloc, god of rain and fertility; and Quetzalcoatl, counterpart of the Maya Kukulcan, god of order, enlightenment, and humaneness, the blond and bearded god, the "Fair God" of romance.

But it is not merely the exteriors of houses that daylight in Tenochtitlan best reveals. Interiors respond to it even more. Here will be seen courts supplied with ponds and fountains, the abode in some instances of wild beasts and birds; chambers, with floors and walls brought to a hard finish by

cement and gypsum, and decked with featherwork
hangings, mats, and cushions, and provided with
low-canopied beds, low tables and stools, flint and
copper implements, and a varied pottery. Between many of the buildings, too, are green garden
plots; and in the lake floating vegetable gardens;
and in the squares, both of Tenochtitlan and Tlatelolco, huge markets in full tide of activity.

Of much interest is all this, but obviously interest of a limited sort. What of the inner self of
the Aztec? What of his soul? As disclosed by his
religion, the soul of the Aztec is dark: war feeds
it and blood anoints it. But art is a second medium of soul disclosure, and through it the soul of
the Aztec is revealed as not inhospitable to light
and beauty. Of Aztec art, featherwork is the most
striking example; but metal work, flower culture,
and poetry are also striking examples — especially
flower culture and poetry. Cempoalla is a place of
roses. Mexico-Tenochtitlan is even more such a
place. Roses peep above the parapets of the communal dwellings and *tecpans*, bloom in the *chinam-
pas* or floating gardens, depend in garlands from
the breasts of idols. No occasion is there that
roses do not grace, be it festival, baptism, wedding,
or funeral; and though the form of arrangement be

oft that of the pyramid or the sacrificial mound, beauty veils the tragedy of the suggestion.

When, therefore, the Aztec poet dreams and sings, it is flowers — roses for the most part — and other things of a flower-like fragility that he celebrates: humming-birds, butterflies, song-birds, and precious stones. "I wonder where I may gather some pretty sweet flowers. Whom shall I ask? Suppose that I ask the brilliant humming-bird . . . suppose that I ask the yellow butterfly. They will tell me." "I polished my noble new song like a shining emerald. I arranged it like the voice of the *Tzinitzcan* bird. . . . I set it in order like the chant of the *Zacuan* bird. I mingled it with the beauty of the emerald, that I might make it appear like a rose bursting its bud." "They led me within a valley to a fertile spot, a flowery spot where the dew spread out in glittering splendor, where I saw lovely fragrant flowers, lovely odorous flowers, clothed with the dew." But even amid songs of rejoicing rarely is there wanting the minor chord, the plaintive strain common to primitive man. "Weeping, I the singer, weave my songs of flowers of sadness." "I lift my voice in wailing, I am afflicted as I remember that we must leave the beautiful flowers, the noble songs." "Only sad flowers and songs are here in Mexico, in Tlatelolco, Ohuaya! Ohuaya!"

The Spaniard beholding Mexico-Tenochtitlan, with its adjunct Tlatelolco, failed to comprehend it, and his failure, save lately and in the case of a few persons, has been our own. The Mexico City or municipality of the Spaniard was, in fact, an Indian pueblo. It had been founded in 1325 by southward roving Indians, the Aztecs, a tribe few in number and near starvation. Finding the rich Mexican valley already occupied, the Aztecs took as their portion the two neighboring islands in Lake Tezcoco, and devoted themselves to their principal need, the production of food, chiefly maize and cacao. The tribe in process of time became fierce, bloody, and prosperous; and it was the struggle for food that made them so.

This struggle for subsistence, indeed, is the key to Aztec life and institutions. To this struggle was it due that the inhabitants of Tenochtitlan planted gardens and invented the floating garden. To this was it due primarily that, feeling the need of controlling communication with the mainland, they built causeways which might be utilized as dikes. To this was it due that, feeling the need of a water supply and of an increased amount of food, they mustered courage and conquered portions of the mainland nearest to them. To this was it due that, growing in population and power and needing yet more food, they forced into existence a tripartite confederacy to levy contribution over an ever-widening area. To this was it due that, discovering the value of terror as a means of rule, they developed the ancient Maya-Nahua cult of human sacrifice — at first practised infrequently — into proportions at once colossal and revolting, and made Huitzilopochtli, the god of war, their local deity in chief.

The Aztec tribe as an organism in embryo had but one head — a sachem or cacique, a civil leader. In him, seemingly, were combined dual elements — the Above or Masculine element, and the Below or Feminine. With expansion and conflict came a need of differentiation of attributes, and there arose the war leader or Chief-of-Men. The distinctively Masculine element was now embodied in him; the Feminine being reserved to his associate, who henceforth bore the title — to many so puzzling — of "Snake Woman." In the days of the Spanish Conquest the Snake Woman, though often alluded to, makes no particular figure. The three overshadowing figures are Chiefs-of-Men —

Montezuma, Cuitlahuatzin, and Quauhtemotzin. Of these Montezuma is reflective and weak; the other two, his successors, decisive and strong.

Just here, however, our account of Mexico-Tenochtitlan must cease, for at the South Causeway, bowing, stands Cortés. He has come with some four hundred men, fifteen horses, and seven light guns. The route by which he traveled from the 31st of August to the 15th of October has been from Xocotlan southwest to Tlascala, a community independent of Montezuma yet distrustful of the Spaniard; and from Tlascala southwest to Cholula. From Cholula, in the valley or plain of Huitzilipan, the invaders have marched west to the mountain ridge connecting Popocatepetl with its mate, Yztaccihuatl, and from here, early in November, have surveyed the basin-like valley of Mexico, with Mexico-Tenochtitlan afar off amid the waters of Lake Tezcoco. They have then approached the border of Lake Chalco, traversed a causeway leading to a peninsula, Itztapalapan, and now, in the community of Itztapalapan itself, stand dazed before the "stone work," the "woodwork of cedar and other sweet scented trees," the "orchard and garden full of roses and fruit trees," and the "pond of fresh water with birds of many kinds and breeds." To Bernal Díaz and his followers, touched with the spirit of Spanish romanticism, the scene appears as the "enchantments of the legend of Amadis."

In the mind of Montezuma, meanwhile, the grave question has been: Can these Spaniards, these strangers of the sunrise, be gods?

When Grijalva's expedition appeared off the coast in 1518, it had been reported to Tenochtitlan that in the "waters of heaven," as the open sea was called, "floating towers" had appeared, from which had descended beings with white faces and hands, with beards and long hair, and wearing raiment of brilliant colors and "round head-coverings." Could these beings be priests or heralds of the Fair God Quetzalcoatl, come, according to the Maya-Nahua tradition, to resume sway over his people? Before proof could be adduced, Grijalva had departed; and then, shortly, had come swift messengers with news of Cortés and with pictures of his "floating towers" and of his fair-visaged yet bearded attendants, handling the thunder and bestriding fierce creatures that spurned the ground.

Proof regarding the quality of the fair strangers

was required now more than ever, and so the first
embassy had been sent to Cortés — the embassy
that had carried back, as a specimen of the round
head-coverings of the strangers, the gilt helmet.
This contrivance, as it chanced, resembled the
head-coverings of the Aztec gods, and especially
of Huitzilopochtli, god of war.   So there had been
sent to Cortés the second embassy, bringing the
head dresses of quetzal feathers.   Now these head-
dresses were those of the four principal gods of
the Aztecs: Tezcatlipoca, god-of-the-breath-of-life;
Huitzilopochtli, god of war; Tlaloc, god of fertility; and Quetzalcoatl, the fair or culture god.
What they seemingly were meant to signify to
Cortés was that Montezuma, tentatively at any
rate, was willing to acknowledge the former as,
like himself, entitled to wear them as a representative of the gods.

Nor was this all that the wonderful gifts of the
second embassy were meant to signify.   Among the
gifts, as will be remembered, were two great wheels
— one of gold, and one of silver.   All Indians of
America possess a social system more or less fully
worked out from the heavenly spaces — the Four
Quarters or cardinal points of direction, and the
three regions — Above, Below, and Center.   The

four head-dresses, symbolizing the four principal gods, may therefore be conceived as meant to stand to Cortés for the Four Quarters; and the gold and silver wheels, respectively, for the Above and the Below. Something of this kind almost certainly was symbolized by the gifts which, besides being in the nature of a bribe to the Spaniard, as a human being, to depart, were likewise in the nature of a propitiatory offering to him, as a god or at least a high priest, to be merciful.

Whether or not the Spaniards really possessed preternatural attributes, it had vastly puzzled all Mexico to decide. The Cempoallans had industriously spread the idea that they did; and one thing only had served to detract from the claim. At Tlascala, where the matter had been put to a test, some of the Spanish horses, those creatures of terror, had been killed, hacked apart, and triumphantly devoured at feasts. At Cholula, however, Cortés by the cleverness of Marina had with unerring precision alighted upon an Aztec plot to destroy him — had, as the marveling Cholulans expressed it, "read their very minds and thoughts"; and such power could pertain to gods alone.

But to come back to the Spanish leader as he stands, bowing, at the South Causeway outside of

Itztapalapan. Whether he be divine or human, it has become apparent that his entry into Tenoch-titlan can no longer be prevented by gifts nor thwarted by guile. Montezuma, therefore, making a virtue of necessity, is about to come forth to greet him. Not that machinations have ceased at all. Once the Spaniards are beyond the draw-bridges with retreat cut off, once securely lodged in one of the principal *toopans*, it is the purpose of the Chief-of-Men, counseled thereto by the dire Huitzilopochtli himself, to destroy the invaders utterly and to send them in batches to the great pyramid as a savory and acceptable blood-offering.

The point where the ceremonies incident to the meeting of Montezuma with Cortés are to take place is on the South Causeway at Acachinanco, a causeway junction, and here a great crowd is gathered. It would seem that not alone is Tenoch-titlan a settlement of four divisions, but that Aztec territory as such, outside of Tenochtitlan, partakes of the same plan; for at the causeway junction Cortés is received by four Aztec subchiefs from Tezcoco, Itztapalapan, Tacuba, and Coyohua-can, settlements on the lake shore to the north-east, southeast, northwest, and southwest, respec-tively, of Tenochtitlan. The lake is crowded with observers in canoes, but the causeway itself, the present Calzada de Iztapalapan, is kept clear, and down the vista which it forms rises Mexico, full of mystery.

The four subchiefs conduct the Spaniards to the point where the South Causeway merges in the South Avenue, the present street El Rastro, leading to the great square, and here Montezuma appears in person. He comes reclining in a sumptuous litter borne upon the shoulders of attendants. At sight of Cortés he descends, and there is spread above him a baldaquin of light greenish-blue feathers with fringe of gold, pearls, and jade. He is a man about fifty-two years old, tall, slender, and of dignified mien, and his hair is worn short over the ears. His garb is a robe of radiant blue and gold, and his feet are shod with golden sandals. Is it as priest of Huitzilopochtli that he thus presents himself to Cortés, the possible representative of that other deity, the Fair God Quetzalcoatl, waiting to dispossess him? Be that as it may, the four subchiefs, habited likewise in heavenly blue, advance to his support. Dignitaries bearing tripartite wands, symbolizing the authority of the Confederacy, go before him, while attendants sweep clean the highway, and even lay carpets that the golden sandals may not touch the ground.

As Montezuma draws near, Cortés dismounts from his horse and steps forward. Montezuma kisses the earth — an act performed by pressing it with the hand and then carrying the hand to the lips — and offers to Cortés — how much of Mexico is here! — a bunch of roses. The Spanish leader moves to salute Montezuma by an embrace, but is restrained by a gesture and instead places about his neck a necklace of beads taken from his own person. Throughout the ceremony the sides of the avenue are lined with attending sages, all of whom are barefoot, and to none of whom is it permitted to raise the eyes to Montezuma — the man of great medicine, the high priest.

When the Spaniards entered Mexico it was November 8, 1519. Between this date and the beginning of 1520, Cortés and his men found lodgings in the halls and chambers of the *tecpan*, the official house or council lodge in the great square, near the great temple, formerly the quarters of Montezuma himself, but now vacated to accommodate the Spaniards; Montezuma having taken up new quarters in one of the vast communal dwellings. Here Cortés made himself secure by placing cannon to command the approaches, and here he was received in audience by Montezuma, who, causing him to be seated on "a very rich platform," in a chamber "facing a court" embellished with fountains and flowers, addressed him thus: "We believe that our race was brought to these parts by a lord, whose vassals they all were, and who returned to his native country. . . . And we have always believed that his descendants would come to subjugate this country and us, as his vassals; and according to the direction from which you say you come, which is where the sun rises, and from what you tell us of your great lord, or king, who has sent you here, we believe and hold for certain that he is our rightful sovereign."

Early fruits of the occupation of the *tecpan* by Cortés were the discovery by accident of the walled-up storeroom containing the official treasure of the Aztec Government — that Aladdin's cave whence had come the gold and silver wheels; the burning alive of certain Aztec plotters; and the seizure of the person of the Chief-of-Men, who, transferred to the *tecpan*, became, under Castilian tutelage, the tool and mouthpiece of his captor.

During 1520 complications for the invaders arose. Cortés contrived the seizure of the war chiefs of Tezcoco and Tlacopan, sub-heads of the Aztec tripartite confederacy, and of the war chiefs of Coyohuacan and Itztapalapan, two of the four sub-heads of the Aztec district itself. Then, further, he forbade human sacrifices. By both these acts he stored up trouble for himself. Trouble, furthermore, developed independently from without. Diego Velásquez, Governor of Cuba and Adelantado of the lands over which Cortés was exercising sway, had at length organized a strong expedition under Pánfilo de Narváez, a man of "hollow" voice, to assert his authority. Narváez reached San Juan de Ulúa in April, and secretly got into relations with Montezuma. In order to check him, Cortés was compelled to divide his own small command. Leaving one hundred and forty men under Pedro de Alvarado in Tenochtitlan, he marched forth with ninety-two men in May, and before the end of the month had, near Cempoalla, met his foe, defeated him, and made him prisoner. Meanwhile in Tenochtitlan, Alvarado, impetuous by nature and roused by tales of conspiracy among the Aztecs fostered by the coming of Narváez, set upon the population while engaged in celebrating the festival of the god Tezcatlipoca and slaughtered them without discrimination and without ruth.

Stunned by the onslaught but rallying promptly, the Mexicans fiercely assaulted the *tecpan* where the Spaniards were housed, and held them in a state of siege till Cortés, informed of their plight by secret messengers, was able to return to their relief. Food was running short, and Montezuma, being appealed to, induced Cortés to liberate the war chief of Itztapalapan, Cuitlahuatzin by name, that he might calm the people and procure it. This was the beginning of the end of the official character of Montezuma. Cuitlahuatzin was henceforth recognized by the clans as Chief-of-Men, and led the Mexicans in desperate attempts to force the Spaniards out of Tenochtitlan.

It was now late June and departure from the lake settlement became imperative for Cortés. In vain did the Spaniards in a hand-to-hand struggle drive the Aztecs from the dizzy summit of the pyramid in the great square. In vain did Montezuma appeal to his countrymen from the roof of the *tecpan*. The Chief-of-Men, no longer such, was reviled to his face; nay more, was assailed by missiles and stricken in the forehead. Within three days he was dead, and on the fourth at midnight his erstwhile jailers stole silently from the *tecpan* into the avenue leading west to the Tacuba

Causeway — shortest of the three routes to the mainland and interrupted by the fewest sluiceways. At first undetected, they had nearly gained the causeway-head, when the night silence re-echoed to a cry — the shriek of a native woman. A signal drum on the pyramid in Tlatelolco at once boomed forth a warning, and secrecy was at an end. It was the *noche triste* — the "doleful night." The bridges over the sluiceways were gone and could not be quickly replaced. Men, horses, and booty, smitten in rear and flank, filled the chasms in a tangled mass. Cortés himself got over by the greatest difficulty. Alvarado, it is said, cleared one of the chasms by an unparalleled vaulting leap. Velásquez de León and Francisco de Morla fell, to emerge no more. Of the total force of Spaniards — 1250 men since the capture of Narváez — some 450 were missing.

Twenty-four horses survived the catastrophe, but the significance of this fact was now small. Neither white stranger nor horse was any longer preternatural. Both were proven mortal; both could perish. Cortés, after all, was not the Fair God Quetzalcoatl — was not even his priest. He was not divine in any sense — just human, just lustful — a dissembling conqueror of flesh and

blood. Once on the mainland, the Spaniards
were able to stay somewhat the Aztec pursuit;
and though, as Cortés expressed it, "without a
horse that could run, or a horseman who could
lift an arm, or a foot soldier who could move,"
he finally managed to round Lake Tezcoco on
the north, and so, after a fierce *mêlée* at Otumba
on the 7th of July, to reach friendly and shelter-
ing Tlascala. Among the saved, besides Alvarado,
were Gonzalo de Sandoval, Cristóbal de Olid, and
the indispensable Marina and Aguilar.

The capture of Tenochtitlan and the reduction
of the Aztecs to submission were still as much as
ever the objects of Cortés, and he resumed the
task sturdily in spite of his temporary check. His
forces he rested and augmented. Surrounding
peoples he coerced or conciliated. The road to
Vera Cruz he put under guard. Disaffection in
his own ranks, due to the presence of so many
of Narváez's men, he quieted by "soothing elo-
quence." At length, on the 28th of December,
all was ready. Tezcoco was occupied, and thirteen
vessels — shallow barges which, after the manner
of Balboa in Darien, had been constructed in the
forest — were carried in pieces across the mountains and launched on Tezcoco Lake. Between

March and May, 1521, the Spaniards seized Itzta-palapan and other points; and, during May and June, Cortés, with nine hundred Spaniards and thousands of native allies, eighty-six horses, and eighteen guns, began a systematic siege of Tenoch-titlan by land and water. Many were the advances and repulses. The Aztecs resisted not alone with determination but with the utmost fury. They cut the great dike; they converted every canal into a moat; they made of every house a castle. Taunts and challenges no less than missiles they flung across the water and down the converging avenues. By night captive Spaniards, goaded to the top of the Tlatelolco Pyramid, were spectacularly slaughtered in the glow of sacrificial fires.

Spanish valor did much toward the reduction of the great community of the lake, but famine and wholesale demolition of buildings did more, and on the 13th of August the Chief-of-Men, Quauhte-motzin, doughty successor to Cuitlahuatzin — who had died of smallpox before the siege — surrendered in despair his own person and what remained of his nation.

So fell Mexico-Tenochtitlan. Fortunate was it for Cortés that in 1519 it was Montezuma who held in Mexico the position of Chief-of-Men! Had it been otherwise — had this position been held by Cuitlahuatzin or Quauhtemotzin — it may be doubted whether the Sun myth of the Fair God and his impending return would have been permitted to paralyze action. In a sense far from fanciful, Montezuma, "sicklied o'er with the pale cast of thought," was the Hamlet of the Aztecs.

CHAPTER V

Gold! Gold! Gold! Gold!
Bright and yellow, hard and cold.
HOOD: *Miss Kilmansegg.*

BALBOA had fallen before Pedrarias, but the search
for some passageway to the provinces and islands
of the South Sea, rich in spices, pearls, and gold,
was continued by not unworthy successors in the
persons of Andrés Niño — a sea-dog not to be
confounded with Pero Alonso Niño, pilot under
Columbus and Ojeda — and Gil Gonzalez Dávila.
Columbus himself had sought this passageway
or strait, between 1502 and 1504, and others had
followed him. This Niño, too, had explored the
coast of Darien in behalf of Balboa. In 1519, the
year of Balboa's death, Niño entered into a partnership with Gil Gonzalez, treasury agent for Española, a man of great practicality and excellent
judgment. The partners were empowered by the
Crown to take over the ships built by Balboa and

139

to make exploration one thousand leagues to the west. Pedrarias — seventy years old, drier, harder, more inflexible than ever — refused to deliver the vessels. Gonzalez, whose rank in the partnership was that of Captain-General, thereupon dismantled his own ships, and, repeating the feat of Balboa, carried the materials over the mountains to the river Balsas. In the end, after delays and discouragements comparable to those of Balboa, he managed to build and equip four small vessels and with them to sail westward on January 21, 1522.

This expedition, which took a double form — a coasting voyage by Niño and a march overland by Gonzalez — came first to the lands of the cacique Nicoya, from whom Gonzalez learned that fifty leagues to the northward there dwelt a greater cacique whose name was Nicaragua. Gonzalez abhorred strife as much as Pedrarias delighted in it, and the naïve wisdom of Nicaragua had therefore a chance to unfold itself unhindered. Whence, asked the cacique, after listening to a detailed account of the Mosaic scheme of creation, did the sun and moon obtain their light and how would they lose it? Why did not the God of the Christians make a better physical world, one more comfortable to dwell in? And finally, speaking in the ear of the interpreter, he asked: "Came these men from the sky?" Being assured that they did, his next query was: "But how? Came they directly down like a spent arrow, or riding a cloud, or in a circuit like a bent bow?"

The Indian community over which Nicaragua ruled was situated on a large freshwater sea, the present Lake Nicaragua, and, striding into it, Gonzalez drank of the water and took possession in the name of the King of Spain. "It is by situation," he wrote, "barely three leagues from the South Sea, and, according to the pilots, connected with the North Sea. If so, it is a great discovery." Here Gonzalez repelled an Indian attack under a picturesque cacique named Diriangen, and, having satisfied himself that as yet the Spaniards of Mexico, Cortés and his followers, had made no southerly advance, returned to Panamá. As for Andrés Niño, he had coasted as far northwestward as the Bay of Fonseca on the shores of the later Central American provinces of Salvador and Honduras.

But what meanwhile of the doings of Pedrarias? It was in January, 1519, that Balboa had been got

rid of, and by the 15th of August Pedrarias and
Espinosa — Gaspar de Espinosa, now Captain-
General of the South Sea — had crossed the Isthmus from Aclá and had founded Panamá to serve
as a southern terminal for the long contemplated
chain of posts to connect the Atlantic with the
Pacific side of the Isthmus until the ardently
desired interoceanic strait should be discovered.
Later the same year a northern terminal was provided through the founding of Nombre de Dios.

With the rise of Panamá, now created by royal
decree a city and the capital of Darien, Santa
María la Antigua, forever ill-famed as the place of
execution of Balboa, sank rapidly to decay and
in September, 1524, was burned by the Indians.
Henceforth, in the old Tierra Firme, Panamá
and Nombre de Dios are the names wherewith
to conjure. About these cities, more than about
any others of the Indies, does romance cling. A
wide road, says Peter Martyr, was built from one
to the other "through mountains overgrown with
thick woods never touched from all eternity," to
the intent that "two carts side by side might pass
over with ease to search ye secrets of either spa-
cious Sea." And "ye secrets" were "searched"
well, for at Panamá, by the middle of the century,

not only did there ride at anchor "ships from the South and far western East, laden with the wealth of half a world," but "in the sun-beaten streets gold and silver lay stacked in bricks," waiting, "along with spices and precious merchandise," transportation to Nombre de Dios.

Pedrarias had made headway also both to the west and east of his new capital. To the west, as far as the nation of the Chiriqui, famed as potters, he had sent Espinosa and Francisco Pizarro, the latter dutiful as ever. To the south he had likewise sent a faithful retainer and honest man, Pascual de Andagoya, who, following the Isthmus of Darien to where it broadens into the continent of South America (Mundus Novus), became the explorer of Birú, whence very possibly the name Pirú, and ultimately that of Perú. At any rate, out of the Andagoya expedition grew, as we shall see, the subsequent and ever memorable enterprise of Pizarro.

Pedrarias's next step was to send Hernández de Córdoba to forestall Gonzalez in the occupation of Nicaragua, a country claimed by him as within the confines of Darien.

Gonzalez appeared at Panamá just when Pedrarias was prepared to appropriate his conquests,

and so Balboa-like had fairly thrust his head between the jaws of the lion; but he was quick enough
to withdraw it, for he spread sail from Nombre de
Dios as Pedrarias rode up in hot haste to intercept
him.   When Gonzalez returned, he approached
Nicaragua from the Honduras coast.   He thus
avoided Pedrarias himself but encountered instead
Hernando de Soto, lieutenant to Córdoba.   Gonzalez defeated Córdoba, but only to succumb to
the superior force of Francisco de las Casas, one
of Cortés's lieutenants, who carried him to Mexico
as a prisoner.

Córdoba meantime, thinking the occasion oppor-
tune, sought to set up an independent government
in Nicaragua and Honduras.   This act of treachery
to Pedrarias was reported to him at Panamá by
De Soto, and in January, 1526, Pedrarias set sail
for Nicaragua in person.   With characteristic
energy and ruthlessness, he arrested Córdoba, put
him to death, and took control of the province.
The death of Córdoba may be regarded as marking
the end of the long-standing duel between Pedrarias and the successors of Balboa, and its conclu-
sion was not unfavorable to the "swarthy-souled"
Governor.

Upon Pedrarias — cunning, indomitable, vindictive — Fortune seemed ever to smile. When, for example, in May, 1520, Lope de Sosa came to Antigua to supersede him in office, that unhappy man was mortally stricken in the cabin of his ship as he prepared to disembark for his inauguration. Again, when in 1526 the Governor was recalled posthaste to Panamá for trial, just as he was on the point of seizing from Cortés himself Honduras as part of Nicaragua, what should befall but, though superseded as to Darien by Pedro de los Ríos, his authority over Nicaragua was confirmed! But the fact is not to be overlooked that he was ably and zealously seconded at Court by his wife, Isabel de Bobadilla, whom he had seasonably dispatched to Spain with his pearls and gold.

The last years of his life, despite the fact that they were the years of an octogenarian, were active and marked by bloodshed. On the caciques of the country who rose in revolt, he wreaked diabolical vengeance by his bloodhounds. But he had withal an eye for trade and transportation. He projected a transcontinental route between Lake Nicaragua and the present Greytown, and afterwards one between León and the north coast by way of Salvador. He became interested in the expedition of Pizarro to Peru, but in this matter

10

he for once suffered bafflement, and died at León, in 1530, as he was nearing his ninetieth year.

If the adventure of Gil Gonzalez to Lake Nicaragua, in 1522–23, was prompted by fear of southward encroachment by Cortés, Cortés himself was not blind to the chance of northward encroachment by the Spaniards of the Isthmus. In other words, the conqueror of Mexico and founder of New Spain sought success also to the south, and for two reasons. There lay the districts of Guatemala and Honduras — districts which, it was said, must "far exceed Mexico in riches, while equaling her in the size of towns, in the number of inhabitants, and in culture." And there, in Castilian fancy, figured that long-sought interoceanic strait upon which every one counted to reach the vast Pacific with its isles of mystery and gold.

If the Spaniards had but known it, Guatemala held things more wonderful than gold or spices or even "soft sensuous pearls," for it had been the seat and center of early Maya culture centuries before, and within its limits, or just beyond, lay the amazing ruins of Tikal, Naranjo, Palenque, and Copan. But for the sixteenth century Span-

iard archeology did not exist. His quest was still
the same as that of Columbus and Behaim, one
still inspired by the lure of treasure.

To make the conquest of Guatemala, Cortés
chose Pedro de Alvarado. Alvarado, of Badajos,
whom we have already met, was of good figure
and engaging countenance. He was athletic, too,
and an excellent horseman, and his hair and beard
were red — so red that the Indians were tempted
to think him Quetzalcoatl, the Fair God, and
christened him the Sun. But though in a sense a
good comrade, Alvarado was easily roused to anger
and to brutal vengeance. He left Mexico City for
Guatemala on December 6, 1523, with one hundred and twenty horsemen, three hundred foot-soldiers, a few pieces of artillery, and a large body of
Mexicans. The principal Guatemalan tribes were
in certain respects superior to the Aztecs and
comparable to the Peruvians. Of their chief
settlements, Utatlan was most celebrated. Mas-
sive official buildings, religious and governmental,
grouped about a court made it rudely magnificent.
The subjugation of these people took the better
part of two years. During this time Alvarado
passed also into Salvador. Here, contrary to his
expectation, he failed to get news of an interoceanic

strait to the southward but heard of distant cities, built of stone and lime and densely populated — an echo, no doubt, of Quito and Cuzco.

Some months later, Alvarado was met by news of a startling character. Cortés, it was declared, had died, not in Mexico but on the way to Honduras, whither he was conducting an expedition. If so, who would be his successor? It might well be Alvarado; and the conquistador at once made ready to repair to the seat of government in New Spain. Cortés was soon discovered to be far from dead, however, for toward the close of 1525 Alvarado received orders from him to repair straightway to Honduras with all his forces. Vehemently declaring that all he possessed he owed to Hernan Cortés, and that with him he would die, Alvarado obeyed. But he learned on crossing the border that his master had changed his plans and had returned by sea to Vera Cruz, whereupon, in the midsummer of 1526, Alvarado retraced his own steps to Santiago, of which he had been a founder. But his venturesome spirit would not let him rest content with his single conquest. Comprehensive ideas had gripped him. He felt the imperious lure of golden dreams. He would go back to Mexico after all. He would see Cortés, secure his support, and sail for Spain. There he would win sanction to adventure where the South beckoned. He would be the man to complete the work of Balboa.

But what of the expedition of Cortés into Honduras? Originally it had not been Cortés's intention to make this expedition in person. He had chosen for the task Cristóbal de Olid, a friend of Velásquez, Governor of Cuba, a "strong limbed" man and "a very Hector in fight." But although Olid sailed from Vera Cruz to Honduras, he had on the way, at Habana, gone back to his allegiance to Velásquez. It had thereupon become necessary to send after the recreant a sleuth in the person of Francisco de las Casas. At Triunfo de la Cruz, just south of Columbus's island of Guanaja, Olid had captured Las Casas and also Las Casas's prisoner, Gil Gonzalez, but had afterwards been mortally stabbed by his captives as he sat with them at meat.

Cortés had been unfaithful to Velásquez; Olid had been unfaithful to Cortés; would Las Casas be any more faithful than Olid had been? Such, in the mind of the Conqueror of Mexico, was now the question. "Villain whom I have reared and trusted," Cortés had exclaimed on hearing of the treachery of Olid, "by God and St. Peter he shall rue it!" As for Las Casas, it were well, perhaps, that he even have not too much the temptation of opportunity. So, late in October, 1524, Cortés set forth for the district of Tabasco, where he planned to cross the peninsula of Yucatán, then thought to be an island, to the northern coast of Honduras. He took a force of about one hundred horsemen and forty foot-soldiers, together with pages, musicians, jugglers, servants, and some three thousand Indians. A unique feature was a body of Aztec war chiefs and caciques from about Lake Tezcoco, including Quauhtemotzin, deposed Chief-of-Men of Tenochtitlan. These it had not been deemed prudent to leave in Mexico in the absence of the Conqueror.

At Teotilac, a point between Iztapan and Lake Peten, Cortés became convinced that the deposed chiefs and caciques in his train were plotting to overthrow him and to restore in Mexico the Aztec régime, and he hanged two of them, Quauhtemotzin and the war chief of Tlacopan, to a ceiba tree at midnight. Thus was tragedy invoked. But comedy did not range far behind. On an island in Lake Peten was a fairly large Indian settlement where Cortés left a badly lamed horse. The Indians, filled with veneration for the strange creature, fed it on flowers and birds, of which diet it speedily died. They then worshiped it in effigy in one of their temples as a god of thunder and lightning, a practice which was still maintained in 1614.

The march to the southeast, begun after the Spanish mode with music and dancing, quickly became a thing of dolor. Rivers, forest-clad morasses, lakes, and labyrinthine sloughs seemed everywhere; and when these at length ceased, there supervened a flinty mountain pass which cost the lives of men and of scores of horses. To the south lay the ruins of Palenque, but they awakened no interest, and it was five weary months before the exhausted band reached Golfo Dulce and the Spanish town of Nito.

At Trujillo, where Cortés was planning yet further conquests, disturbing news overtook him. Quarrels had broken out among members of the administrative board to which he had left the government, and upon rumor of his death his property had been seized. His presence was sorely needed to save his fortune and his conquests. Resolving to return, he set out on April 25, 1526, and reached Vera Cruz late in May, so emaciated and broken in body as to be but a specter of his

former self. In Mexico City — now a "city" in
the true sense of the term — Cortés was welcomed
with demonstrations of delight by Spaniards and
Indians alike. He was still to all beholders the
Spanish conquistador *par excellence.*

Like Columbus, Cortés was an object of much
envy on both sides of the Atlantic, and to make
clear his doings to the Spanish King he took ship
in 1528 for Spain. He debarked at Palos, where
he is said to have met Pizarro; and in his train,
by a freak of fate, was Pizarro's future Brutus,
Juan de Rada. Charles V was at this time holding
Court at Toledo, and here Cortés was met and
escorted into his monarch's presence by a brilliant
group of nobles. Needless to say, he did not come
empty handed. Indeed, by comparison with what
he brought, the offerings of Columbus to Ferdinand and Isabella seem mean and trivial. First,
there was heaped treasure of gold and silver; then
featherwork and embroidery; then specimens of
arms and implements; strange plants and animals
and beautiful birds. Imposing Indian chiefs, among
them a son of Montezuma, graced his retinue,
while amusement was contributed to the occasion
by dwarfs, albinos, and human monstrosities. Cortés, like Columbus, would have knelt at the royal

feet, but Charles, like Ferdinand and Isabella, raised up the suppliant and compelled him to speak sitting; and, when illness overtook him, the King personally visited him in his lodgings.

In Spain the conqueror of Mexico contracted a brilliant marriage. Catalina, his first wife, had already died, and Marina, his Indian mistress, he had given as wife to one of his soldiers. He received the title of Marqués del Valle de Oaxaca (Marquis of the Valley) and was made a Knight of Santiago. But amid these marks of royal favor misfortunes were not wanting. His father had died, and so had his beloved follower, the youthful Gonzalo de Sandoval. Capping all, he failed of his ambition to be made a duke, a glory which he coveted beyond any other.

CHAPTER VI

PIZARRO AND THE INCAS

He that has partners has masters.—Pope Sixtus V.

IN the same year in which Cortés started for Honduras, Francisco Pizarro set out for the Birú country of Andagoya. Under Balboa, on the shores of the Gulf of San Miguel, he had heard of Birú as the gateway to a country far to the south where the people were rich and used ships and beasts of burden; and later, under Morales, he had paid in this quarter a hasty and bloody visit. Pizarro, native of Trujillo in Estremadura, — tall, shapely, sedate — was at this time about fifty-three years old. He undoubtedly was ambitious but he certainly was not inspired. His strength lay not in initiative but in dogged persistence and endurance. His conquest of Peru was in certain respects heroic, but it was not original. His plans, so to speak, were borrowed ready finished from Cortés.

154

Pizarro had three coadjutors or partners: Diego de Almagro, an old friend and fellow rancher in the Isthmus; Fernando de Luque, vicar of Panamá; and Pedrarias Dávila, the Governor. To the requirements of military command Pizarro was equal; but Almagro was needed to superintend the dispatch of supplies, and Luque to play softly the part of intercessor with Pedrarias. None of the triumvirate was young in years; but none had as yet won a fortune, and, as Sir Arthur Helps sagely remarks, the disappointed are ever young. Young in this sense, and withal energetic, Pizarro, Almagro, and Luque certainly were, for between mid-November in 1524 and the end of the year 1528 they succeeded in demonstrating both the actuality and attainability of that Golden Peru which had been the objective of Balboa. In accomplishing this, however, never perhaps did men suffer more.

Starting from Panamá with one vessel, some eighty men, and four horses, Pizarro touched at the Pearl Islands and stopped for six weeks at Puerto de la Hambre (Hunger Harbor) while the ship went back to the Pearl Islands for supplies. Meanwhile Almagro had sailed from Panamá with a second ship and seventy men, and had sought for

Pizarro as far as Puerto de la Hambre and the river San Juan. But the latter, ere this, had retraced his course to a spot in Tierra Firme called Chicamá, and here Almagro finally overtook him. By this time both leaders had endured much. Almagro had lost an eye by an arrow, and Pizarro had nearly starved to death.

It was at this stage of affairs that Pedrarias permitted himself to be outmaneuvered. He was preparing to enter Nicaragua and was loath to spare men to Pizarro and Almagro. In fact, he was on the point of ordering "the dutiful one" back to Panamá for good, so little did he perceive the glitter of gold in his direction, when his purpose was stayed by the persuasiveness of Luque and the resourcefulness of Almagro.

Though Pizarro might not be intellectual, and though of a surety he was unlettered, he nevertheless was astute. Amid his own active misery and that of his men he was shrewd enough to keep personally beyond the reach of the Governor at Panamá. Not for nothing had he served the latter all these years. He knew his Pedrarias. So it was Almagro and not Pizarro who went to Panamá, persuaded Pedrarias, for a consideration, to relinquish his share in the enterprise to Gaspar de

Espinosa, and returned with two ships, and with
arms and supplies, to resume the great adventure
to the south.

The two leaders now had with them an unusual
man, one "dextrous in his wit" — the pilot Bartolomé Ruiz. The trio, with one hundred and
sixty followers, sailed to the river San Juan and
there separated. Almagro returned to Panamá
for more men; Pizarro held the ground gained —
holding gains was ever a Pizarro trait; and Ruiz
navigated the coast of Mundus Novus to the southwest. By this allotment of parts, opportunity —
the spectacular chance — was all with Ruiz, and
he perceived his advantage. Pushing boldly to
and beyond the equator — the first navigator so
to do in the Pacific — he rent the veil from before
Peru. That is to say, he discovered the Island of
Gallo and Bay of San Mateo, and, coming upon
a raft propelled by a lateen sail and manned by
Indians, he learned of Tumbez and also of Cuzco,
where ruled the Inca and where there was vast
golden treasure.

The crucial hour in the Peruvian expedition
came with the return of Ruiz to the river San
Juan, bringing tidings of what he had seen and
heard; and it was an hour exalted by the heroism

of Pizarro. Almagro had obtained about forty
men in Panamá, but it was realized that the Peruvians were numerous and organized and that a
strong force would be required to overcome them.
So back once more to Panamá went Almagro.
There Pedro de los Ríos governed in the stead of
Pedrarias, but he was hardly more willing to supply
men to Pizarro and Almagro than Pedrarias had
been, for the men already with Pizarro, now withdrawn to the Island of Gallo, had succeeded in
making it known that they were being led to certain and probably futile death.

> Look out, Señor Governor,
> For the drover while he's near,

they wrote in characteristic Spanish doggerel, re-
ferring to Almagro;

> Since he goes home to get the sheep
> For the butcher [Pizarro] who stays here.

Ríos, in fact, insisted upon sending two ships in
command of a jurist, Pedro Tafur, to bring home
the men thus complaining. Still — and here the
value of Luque in the partnership strongly appears — the orders to Tafur were not so drastic

but that Pizarro might proceed with the expedition with such men as chose to abide the issue.

On the Island of Gallo, therefore, Pizarro, upon the arrival of Tafur, assembled his men and put the situation squarely before them. On the one hand lay peril with possible riches; on the other, safety with assured poverty. The choice was theirs. Whether the Spanish chieftain actually drew in the sand with the point of his sword a line to the south of which he dramatically bade those pass who would follow him, is much to be doubted; but in imposing upon his men an unequivocal choice, he did something very like it. At all events, some sixteen men, including Ruiz the pilot, Pedro of Candia, a Greek, and an unnamed negro, stepped to his side; and with this little company Pizarro crossed from Gallo to the smaller but more easily defended Island of Gorgona to await the coming of Almagro preparatory to advancing toward Tumbez. On little Gorgona, "in a cloud-curtained sea, near a fearfully fascinating shore," for seven months he waited, starving.

The topography of primitive Mexico was impressive enough: a low-lying Atlantic seaboard; a gradual rise through tropical vegetation and life to a plateau seventy-four hundred feet above sea-level; guarding this plateau, a mountain wall accentuated by twin volcanic peaks seventeen thousand feet high; and within the wall, covering the plateau in considerable part, a cluster of lakes fresh and salt. But magnificent as was the Mexican scenery, in Peru, Nature, overpassing the impressive, became stupendous and sublime. The Peru of the Incas at the coming of Pizarro stretched along the Pacific coast of South America from the River Ancasmayu, north of Quito in Ecuador, to the River Maule, below Santiago in Chile, a region some twenty-seven hundred miles in length and comprehending the modern States of Ecuador, Peru, and Bolivia, with part of Chile and Argentina. Its main features within the limits of Peru proper — the Peru of today — were an arid ocean strand less than one hundred miles in breadth; a double, at times treble, cordillera or mountain chain — the Andes — from one to two hundred miles in breadth; and a district of tropical forest conserving the sources of the Amazon. To these features should be added the Antarctic, or Humboldt, Current, flowing up the western shore, a current so cold as to shroud the coast in mists and infuse a chill through even the tropics.

The mere walls of the Andes at their ordinary
elevation attained fourteen thousand feet and more.
Then there were giant peaks ranging between
seventeen and twenty-two thousand feet; and, on
the verge of the Inca dominion, Aconcagua, chief
of the Andean giants, to which nearly twenty-
three thousand feet must be assigned. Mere altitude, however, was not in Peru the engrossing
element in the sublime. That element was aloof-
ness — a weird and stern inhumanity to which all
observers have borne witness. "Savage solitudes";
"somber grandeur"; "strange weirdness"; "awe-
inspiring vastness"; "solemn immensity"; "a
waste land where no man goes, or hath gone since
the making of the world!" — such are the words
of description used.

But the grim topography of ancient Peru had
its redeeming feature — sunlight — first on the
mountain tops and then on the surface of Lake
Titicaca. The lake — today about the size of
Lake Erie, but in places some six or seven hundred feet deep, very irregular in shape, and studded
with islands — lay within the plateau of Peru and
Bolivia at an elevation of about thirteen thousand
feet, the largest body of fresh water in the world
at so great an elevation.

11

The light of the sun in the Titicaca Valley gave rise in the course of ages to the barbarism or semi-civilization of the Inca mode of life; but far earlier it gave rise to the Peruvian stage of development in the Megalithic or Great Stone period. "The Sun," to quote a Peruvian writer of Inca descent, "placed his children near the Lake of Titicaca." How long after the Stone Age the age of the Incas came is a question — several centuries, no doubt. Suffice it to say that the Megalithic folk were one day overthrown by invaders from the south, and the remnant of them took refuge, as is now conjectured, in an inaccessible canyon in the valley of the Urubamba River, northwest of the site of Cuzco. Here, at Tampu Tocco (Machu Picchu?), a city peering thousands of feet down upon roaring rapids, the Incas were bred, and in due time — somewhere about the twelfth century — became strong enough to leave their fastness, retake possession of the Titicaca region, and begin that movement of conquest and organization which, with Cuzco as a center, resulted in an empire vaster than was ruled from Moscow or Aix-la-Chapelle, from Bagdad or Granada.

At the coming of Pizarro, the distinctive features of Peruvian culture — features wherein it

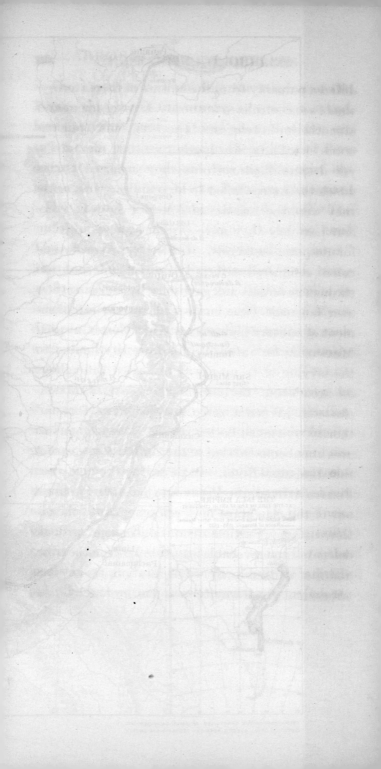

differed palpably from the culture of the Aztecs —
were two: centralized authority in government and
monotheism in religion. The Peruvians (Quichua
tribes) were a far less hardy race than the Aztecs,
yet despite their softness they achieved things
which the Aztecs failed to accomplish.   In a sense
they were the Asiatics of America; both actively
and passively they gave evidence of an aptitude
for despotic statecraft. Unlike the Aztecs, they
ruled conquered tribes by direct interposition
through governors and garrisons; by imposing their
own language (Quichua); and by the establishment of military highways. When Cortés invaded
Mexico, Aztec authority, an authority limited to
the levying of tribute, was respected throughout
an area about the size of the State of Massachusetts. When Pizarro invaded Peru, Inca authority was much better respected throughout an
area about equal to that of the United States east of
the Mississippi River. In a word, by the time when
Pizarro arrived, the Peruvians had largely passed
out of the clan stage of development into the national stage. Particularism, or localism, with its
delegated and revocable leadership within the tribe,
and its leadership by confederation as between
tribes, had given way to incipient monarchy.

The Peruvian religion, like the religion of Old Persia, centered in the worship of the Sun. And, forsooth, what more natural than that the orb to which in peculiar measure the culture of Peru owed its existence should become the chief object of the adoration of the Peruvian tribesman! "The dawn — was it not Birth to him? The mid-day splendor — was it not Power to him? The sunset — typified it not Death to him?" The Inca himself was Sun-begotten, and, being so, bore divine attributes. No Indian official in North America or in South — in Florida, in Mexico, or in Mundus Novus — could compare in rank with the Inca, politically a king and religiously a god.

Centralization of governmental authority in Peru is decisively shown by the social organization which prevailed. The primary unit was the family of five persons, and thence greater units were derived by multiplying by ten until there was obtained the ultimate unit of fifty thousand, the head of which was directly responsible to the Inca. Clanship, however, though outgrown politically, survived economically, for land belonged to the local community and not to the family or individual. In agriculture the Peruvians were adept.

They produced the finest of cotton, and grew excellent maize and potatoes. They made use of the vicuña and the alpaca as sources of the finest wool. But, like all things Peruvian, farming was rigidly supervised and controlled from Cuzco, the produce being divided into three equal parts, whereof two went to the state and one only to the producer.

Countless were the ways in which Inca rule made itself felt. Everybody was enumerated; everybody must dwell in a fixed district and follow a fixed occupation; and, in order that the multitude of tribes incorporated into the nation might readily be distinguished, each tribe must use a distinctive dress and method of wearing the hair. Caste too was universal. Below the Inca and constituting a nobility were lords, priests, warriors, and civil governors; and below the nobility, constituting commoners, were shepherds of llamas, hunters, farmers, and artificers.

The softness which characterized the Peruvians physically, characterized them also intellectually. They excelled in the arts — in pottery, in weaving, and in the fashioning of gold, silver, and bronze. Literature they produced in the form of dramas, love songs, and hymns of worship — of worship,

at times, of something more universal than the
Sun:

> Oh hear me!
> From the sky above,
> In which thou mayest be,
> From the sea beneath,
> In which thou mayest be,
> Creator of the world,
> Maker of all men!

But they evolved no system of writing; not even a
pictographic one, using only knotted and twisted
cords, called *quipus*, to perpetuate their thoughts.
At the time of the Spanish conquest of America
there was more promise for the future in the Hel-
lenic-like barbarism, plastic though crude, of the
Aztecs, than in the Asiatic-like barbarism, rigid
though polished, of the Peruvians.

But what of Francisco Pizarro, Pedro de Candia,
and the others of Pizarro's band whom we left
facing starvation on the little Island of Gorgona
off the coast of Ecuador, and awaiting the coming
of Almagro from Panamá with reinforcements?
Ruiz the pilot was not with them, for he had returned north with Tafur. At the end of seven
months, however, he came in Almagro's stead, and

the company set out, as Pizarro had planned, for Tumbez, which is situated on the gulf later called Guayaquil.

Their course took them past Cape Pasado, the limit of Ruiz's exploratory voyage, past the volcanic peaks of Cotopaxi and Chimborazo, and in twenty days they reached Tumbez. Here Pizarro sent ashore parties under Pedro de Candia and others. The messengers were greeted as superior beings, very much as Cortés and his followers were greeted at San Juan de Ulúa. Their faces were fair; they wore long beards; and their identity as Children of the Light, that Light which in Peru meant so much, was considered established. With them, however, on one occasion went the negro, and to fit him into satisfactory relations with the emissaries of the Dawn was found difficult. They tried washing, but to no effect; and the Peruvians were obliged to accept him for what he was — one not to be understood but simply to be enjoyed. The report of Pizarro's messengers as to what was to be seen at Tumbez — a fortress, a temple, comely Virgins of the Sun, vases of gold — abundantly confirmed the earlier report of Ruiz, but Pizarro had few men (the new Governor at Panamá had seen to that) and he resolved to betake himself directly to Spain to lay his discovery before the King.

There he arrived early in 1528, accompanied by the Greek, Pedro de Candia.   By the 26th of July, at Toledo, he had met Charles V, who created him Governor of all he might discover for a distance of two hundred leagues "to the south of Santiago," a river entering the sea just below the latitude of the Island of Gallo.   The King made Almagro and Luque the Captain and the Bishop of Tumbez; Bartolomé Ruiz, Grand Pilot of the South Sea; Pedro de Candia, Chief of Artillery; and the heroes of the Isle of Gorgona, knights and cavaliers.

From Toledo, Pizarro went to Trujillo, his native town, and drew to his support his brothers, Hernando, Juan, Gonzalo, and Martín of Alcantara, all capable, all brave, and all except the first described as, "like Pizarro himself, illegitimate, poor, ignorant, and avaricious."   The proposed expedition to Peru, unlike the expeditions of prior Spanish adventurers, did not attract followers; and it was with only one hundred and eighty men and thirty horses that in December, 1531, a year after his return from Spain, the Estremaduran was able to set sail with three ships from Panamá for Tumbez.

In the Peruvian conquest there may be said to have been three definite stages: one of waiting and preparation; one of active hostilities; and one of accomplishment. The stage of waiting and preparation, of patience and endurance, has already been glanced at. Here Pizarro shone. From the days when, under Ojeda, Balboa, and Pedrarias, he had served on the terrible Isthmus, to those when he challenged riches and renown on the hardly less terrible coast of Peru, there was nothing that he did not suffer. At San Juan River, toils of the jungle within reach of the hideous dangling boa and of the stealthy alligator; on the Island of Gallo, nauseating food, thunder, lightning, and torrential rain; on Gorgona, plague of insects, incessant, intolerable, inescapable. All these things, with starvation often added, Pizarro suffered, but though in distress he did not repine but bravely endured.

Tumbez he reached in the spring of 1532, and here the invaders were joined by Hernando de Soto with one hundred men and fifty horses from Nicaragua. Thus reënforced, Pizarro, as a means of establishing himself in the country he had set out to despoil and convert, resolved to found a town. Choosing a site near the sea, some thirty

leagues to the south of Tumbez, he founded San
Miguel, the first European settlement in the domain ruled by the Incas. Having secured a base,
the next step was to locate and appraise the forces
of opposition. He accordingly sent De Soto, with
a party of horse, along the foot of the first of the
several great chains of the Andes, to gather information. What Pizarro learned was that in Peru
there was at that time a legitimate ruler named
"Cuzco, son of old Cuzco," and that he had a
brother, Atahualpa, who was in rebellion but to
whom Fortune had been so far favorable that he
had defeated young Cuzco and gone on conquering
the land southward to a place called Caxamarca.
Caxamarca, Pizarro learned, was beyond the
mountain wall which confronted him, but at a
distance of only twelve or fifteen days' march.

Traditionally the first Inca of Peru was Manco
Ccapac, who flourished about 1100 and built or
rebuilt the town of Cuzco. Historically, however, the first Inca was Viracocha, whose reign fell
somewhere about 1380. In 1500 the Inca was
Huayna Ccapac — the "old Cuzco" of Pizarro's
informants — and under him it was that the Inca
dominion was projected northward beyond Quito
and southward into Chile. Huayna Ccapac, "old

Cuzco," was succeeded by his legitimate son Huascar, young Cuzco. But Huascar had a brother, Atahualpa, son of Huayna by a concubine, daughter of the last independent ruler of Quito, and, in order to secure to him a share in the succession, Huayna at his death divided the royal possessions, assigning to Atahualpa the Quito inheritance and to Huascar the remainder. The results usual under such circumstances followed: strife between the brothers arose, and in the contest not only had Atahualpa triumphed but he had succeeded in making Huascar captive.

As between Pizarro and Atahualpa the situation was quite like that which a dozen years before had obtained between Cortés and Montezuma. In both instances, invaders, believed to be engendered of the Sea or dropped from the Sky, sought from a seaboard base to overcome rulers established in the mountains as protectors of capitals which were believed to be the repositories of untold wealth. There were, however, certain differences. The way to Atahualpa, barred as it was by the mighty outer wall of the Andes, was more difficult than the way to Montezuma. But, offsetting this, Cortés's advance was hindered by every subtlest art of Indian subterfuge, while that of Pizarro was uninterfered with.   Then again, Montezuma had, as he thought, laid for Cortés a trap in Mexico-Tenochtitlan itself; whereas Atahualpa, for aught that appears, received Pizarro at Caxamarca with such sublime faith in his own abounding resources that he felt for him little other than contempt.   But let the narrative disclose its own tale.

It was in September that Pizarro set out from San Miguel.   His force was in all one hundred and seventy-seven men, sixty-seven of whom were horsemen.   At first the country was comparatively level, watered by mountain-fed aqueducts, and set with orchards and fields of waving grain. Withal the air was sweet with the breath of flowers, and the people were friendly.   But the soldiers, some of them, showed discontent; and to meet it Pizarro promptly sent back to San Miguel nine men who lacked heart for the great enterprise.

Cortés, under more trying circumstances, had dealt with disaffection by scuttling his ships and by meting out drastic punishments.   Yet to the men of Cortés the evidence of riches ahead was far stronger than to the men of Pizarro, for the latter had beheld naught to compare with the gold and silver wheels presented to Cortés by Montezuma.

To Pizarro, therefore, relieved of his disaffected element but facing mountains and with no treasure in sight, it remained to urge forward his command by appealing to their piety — their sense of duty as propagandists of the Faith. Besides being primitive, proud, and romantic, the Spaniard, it will be recalled, was devout. Devoutness, indeed, as a spur to action, held with him a place second only to avarice.

Pizarro's chief obstacle was the Andes, with "their crests of snow glittering high in the heavens — such a wild chaos of magnificence and beauty as no other mountain scenery in the world [could] show." Up this barrier struggled foot-soldiers and horsemen, the latter dismounted and tugging at their beasts. Here the path hugged the base of a toppling cliff; there it shunned a reeling abyss; while ever above the crawling Spanish line hung, greedy for mishap, that obscene bird of carrion, the Peruvian condor. Near the summit of the range the invaders came upon one of the military roads of the Incas, a road which connected Cuzco with Quito, and which in point of length has been likened to a conceivable highway connecting Calais with Constantinople. It was a road, however, upon which no wheel turned, for, unlike the early

Chaldeans, Babylonians, and Egyptians, the Peruvians, with whom "everything stopped short," were unacquainted with the principle of the wheel.

On this journey upward to Caxamarca, this New World anabasis, Pizarro was met and waited upon, as Cortés had been on his journey, by successive embassies. One came under the escort of De Soto, whom the Spanish leader had sent to reconnoiter, and met Pizarro at the foot of the range; while the others, whereof there were two, met him near the summit. All brought gifts: the first, an elaborate drinking-cup of stone, woolen stuffs embroidered in gold and silver, and perfume; the second, several llamas; and the third, Peruvian sheep, chicha or "fermented juice of the maize," to employ a delicate periphrasis, and, what to the Spaniards was more to the point, "golden goblets" from which to quaff this beverage. Mid-November was now at hand and Pizarro had bested his great obstacle. He had scaled the Andes. Beneath him spread a valley, stream-traversed and highly cultivated, and in this valley he descried three things: the town of Caxamarca, steam rising from hot mineral springs, and — did his pulse quicken? — "a white cloud of pavilions covering the ground as thick as snowflakes."

Pizarro entered Caxamarca on the 15th of November at the hour of vespers. His first act was to send De Soto with twenty horsemen to announce to Atahualpa his arrival; and his second, to send his brother Hernando after De Soto with twenty more horsemen as a reënforcement. The Inca, a man of thirty, sat at the door of his tent, cross-legged on a low cushion, surrounded by male and female attendants. He wore a tunic and robe, but what distinguished him as a ruler was the head-dress, the *borla*. This consisted of a fringed cord of red vicuña wool wound several times around the head, the fringe depending over the eyes. As lord of both Quito and Cuzco, and especially of Quito through his mother, Atahualpa would no doubt have felt himself entitled to wear (as later he did wear) the insignia of Quito, a string of royal emeralds. Seated on his cushion, the Inca held his eyes fixed upon the ground; nor did he raise them or otherwise respond when Hernando Pizarro, with grave Spanish mien, invited him to visit his brother in the town. His thoughts — what were they? In all probability the question in the mind of Montezuma in the case of Cortés: Were these newcomers gods?

It was the horse, as we have seen, that more than

aught else in Indian eyes gave to the Spaniard the seeming of a god. Atahualpa had kept himself informed regarding this weird creature, and in a measure was fortified against the terror of him. Through messengers from the Quito country he had learned that the Spaniard and his horse were not "all one animal," for on the coast a rider had been observed to fall from a horse. Confirming this idea of the separability of horse and rider, had come news that at night the horses were unsaddled. Nor was the horse immortal, for a cacique of the neighborhood of San Miguel had sent word that he personally had killed one.

Glancing up at length from his reverie, Atahualpa said to Hernando Pizarro that the Spaniards could be no great warriors, for the San Miguel *curaca* (cacique) had killed three, besides a horse. Nettled at this speech so weighed and measured in its audacity, Hernando Pizarro replied that one horse, let alone riders, could conquer the whole country; and, as if practically to substantiate the claim, De Soto, the best mounted man in the Spanish group, struck spurs into his steed, dashed across the plain, and, wheeling in graceful circles, reined in the animal so close to the Inca that foam from his sides bespattered the royal garments. But Atahualpa, self-schooled against terror of the horse, did not flinch. To him evidently the Spaniards, if gods at all, were not formidable ones; and when he consented, as now he did, to visit Pizarro in camp the next day, it was, as the chronicle has it, "with the smile of a man who did not very much esteem us."

That night the Spaniards knew fear. The twinkling distant camp fires of the Peruvian host — fires likened in multitude to the stars of heaven — impressed them with a sense of their numerical inferiority, and again Pizarro found it expedient to warm their zeal and stiffen their courage by appealing to them as sons of the Church and propagandists of the Faith. As for Pizarro himself, he had a plan which had been long in his mind: he would seize the person of Atahualpa, even as Cortés had seized the person of Montezuma, and all would be well.

The town of Caxamarca itself was not large. Its distinguishing feature, however, was an extensive triangular plaza — "larger than any plaza in Spain" — enclosed on two sides by long low buildings. These buildings may have been communal dwellings, for they are spoken of as divided on the interior into blocks, each block comprising a suite

12

of rooms. If the buildings in question were communal, they serve to illustrate Peruvian nation-making as in this quarter something yet in process, the clan here not having been superseded by the family. But there were other buildings — survivals of the early medicine lodge and council lodge — temples and great halls, all very much as in Mexico-Tenochtitlan.

Of the great halls there were three, each giving through a wide opening upon the plaza. In one, Pizarro stationed a squadron of horsemen under Hernando Pizarro; in another, a squadron under De Soto; and in the third, a squadron under a doughty cavalier, newly arrived, Sebastián de Benalcazar. The foot-soldiers as a body he placed in concealment round about; but twenty such, picked for their prowess, he attached to his own person, taking with them a central station, well concealed, whence he could sally forth in any direction. Pedro de Candia, be it added, trained upon the plaza, from a "fortress" above it, the artillery of the invaders — two falconets.

Such was the disposition of the Spanish leaders when, about noon of the 16th of November, Atahualpa emerged from his camp on his way to visit Pizarro in Caxamarca, the lion in his lair. He was attended by thousands, and the spectacle offered was that of Montezuma advancing to meet Cortés. But when within a short distance of the town, what should the Peruvian monarch do but stop the progress and prepare to pitch his tents! This Pizarro saw with dismay, for his men, long kept at high tension, must speedily find relief in action or succumb to fear. He accordingly dispatched an earnest request to Atahualpa that he resume the march and enter the town that evening, where every arrangement for his reception and entertainment had been made.

The Inca granted this request and just before sunset the "Child of the Sun" passed the gates. In front, as with Montezuma, came runners, clearing the way of dirt and obstructions and singing sonorous songs — songs pronounced "hellish" in the chronicle. Then came dancers. Then caciques of divers grades bearing "hammers" of silver or copper, and conspicuous for checkered or white liveries. Those immediately about the Inca were caciques or noblemen of special dignity, wearing head-dresses ornamented with gold and silver, breast armor of gold plates, and great ear-studs. All more or less seem to have been distinguished by vestments of blue — that azure (*azul* or sky color) so marked and evidently so significant in the apparel of Montezuma.

The Inca himself, like the "Chief-of-Men," was borne aloft in a litter. He sat on a throne of gold within a baldaquin lined with the brilliant plumage of the parrakeet and covered with gold and silver plates. A man of vigor — large, with bold eyes somewhat bloodshot — his aspect was commanding and even fierce. As lord of Quito, he wore the royal emeralds. As Child of the Sun, he wore the *borla;* and in addition a golden diadem garnished with the wing feathers of the *caraquenque.* It was his right, moreover, to be preceded by a standard bearer carrying a banner emblazoned with the rainbow. In any event he was an impressive figure, as, dividing to the right and left, his numerous escort fell away, leaving him alone, the observed of all observers in the plaza.

No Spaniard was in sight, and Atahualpa was perplexed. "What has become of these fellows?" he demanded with impatience. Hereupon Pizarro sent forth to meet the Indian ruler, and to account to him for the presence of the Spaniards in his country, the priest and spiritual leader of the expedition, Vicente de Valverde, later Bishop of Cuzco. Valverde of course could speak to Atahualpa

only through the interpreter, a young Indian captured at Tumbez, named Fellipillo or Little Philip,
who was for the purpose a feeble dependence, in no
sense a second Marina or Aguilar.   What Father
Valverde undertook to impress upon Atahualpa
was that there was one true God; that He had
sent to earth his Son Jesus Christ; that Christ, being put to death, had left his power in the hands
of St. Peter, who, dying, had passed it on to the
Popes of Rome.   One of the Popes, the one now
alive, had heard that the Indians of the world,
instead of worshiping the true God, "adored idols
and likenesses of the devil."   Thereupon he had
given it into the hands of "Charles, King of Spain
and Monarch of the whole earth," to "conquer the
Indian nations" and bring them to "the knowledge of God and the obedience of the Church."
To effect this conquest, Charles had commissioned "Don Francisco Pizarro — now here."
"If thou shalt deny and refuse to obey," fer-
vently exclaimed the priest, "know that thou
shalt be persecuted with fire and sword without
mercy!"

What Atahualpa probably gathered out of this
harangue, as rendered in what has been called
the "deplorable Cuzcan" of Fellipillo, was that

a distant mysterious lord — a "white stranger's" lord — operating as the agent of a mysterious deity — or of several such, for the Trinity had figured in the discourse — claimed his allegiance and tribute and meant to deprive him and the people of independence. Fear of the Spaniards as themselves gods, or at least preternatural beings, does not seem to have much dwelt in the mind of the Inca, for observing that Father Valverde held in his hand a book, the Bible, whence he had derived the matter of his exhortation, Atahualpa demanded to see it. It was clasped, and the Indian was unable to open it. The priest stepped to the side of the litter to give help. but Atahualpa, resenting the intrusion, forced the clasps back, ran his eyes helplessly through the leaves, and cast the holy volume violently upon the ground.

Not only did the Inca spurn the Word of God, but he at the same time said that he knew how the Spaniards had maltreated his people all the way from Tumbez, even to burning some of them alive, and that he required reparation. Here then was defiance complete — defiance of all the Powers: of the Powers Temporal as well as of those Spiritual; of Emperor, and of Francisco Pizarro, as well as of God, Christ, St. Peter, and the Pope; and punishment was called for. The hour — the moment — had come!

On hearing Father Valverde's report, Pizarro informed his brother Hernando. The latter in turn informed Pedro de Candia, who discharged his falconets — the signal agreed upon — and the horsemen everywhere burst from cover. In advance of all, sword in hand, and shouting "Santiago," ran Pizarro. His object was the royal litter, but ere he could reach it the attendants of Atahualpa had interposed themselves, and there ensued a furious *mêlée*. In the end, amid great slaughter, the litter was overturned and Atahualpa, the god-descended, his robes in tatters, diadem and *borla* torn from his brow, was dragged forth a captive.

Montezuma fell before Cortés, a victim of vacillation, the result of timidity bred of superstition. Atahualpa fell before Pizarro, a victim of assurance which was the result of arrogance. Entering Caxamarca late in the day, Atahualpa had notified Pizarro that he would spend the night within its gates, but with only a fraction of his forces, and these "unarmed." What need, forsooth, of arms, of copper-pointed spears, of bows and arrows, and of lassos, had Atahualpa? Was he not Inca? Was he not literally Child of the Sun? "Your God," he is said to have boasted to Father Valverde, "was, you say, slain by men, the work of his hands; my god," pointing proudly to the sinking Sun, "dies but to live again!"

That November evening, 1532, Pizarro and Atahualpa supped together. Breaking bread with the defeated seems to have been an amiable if somewhat ironical Spanish custom, whether those so honored were themselves Spaniards or not. Cristóbal de Olid had supped with his prisoners Gil Gonzalez and Francisco de las Casas, but only to have his hospitality requited by slashes at his throat. In the case of Atahualpa such requital was not to be apprehended. The Inca was too dazed to think of trying it himself, and his followers were too profoundly overawed. But, dazed though Atahualpa was, he did not so remain. On the morrow after his overthrow he noticed that, while the Spaniards brought in as booty many bales of beautifully woven woolen and cotton fabrics, the things which as booty they esteemed most were the royal utensils of gold and silver. If it were gold and silver the white strangers coveted — he personally much preferred glass — these metals abounded in Peru. Why not purchase with them his own

freedom? Freedom was valuable to him just
then, for the legitimate Inca, Huascar his brother,
was himself a captive, and when the latter should
learn of the captivity of Atahualpa, what plots —
plots even with the invaders — might he not con-
coct against him? One day, therefore, as he and
Pizarro stood in a chamber of Pizarro's quarters,
he suddenly offered to cover the floor with gold if
his freedom were granted.

The offer provoked only a smile, and Atahualpa
was piqued. He stepped proudly to the wall, and
indicating a point thereon as high as he could
reach, offered to fill the entire room to that point
with gold. He also offered to fill a smaller room,
adjoining, twice over with silver. The only conditions he made were that the metals should not
first be melted down, but should retain the form
of the objects into which they had been wrought,
and that he should have two months within which
to fulfill his undertaking.

Then ensued one of the most wonderful episodes
in history. Each day there went forth from the
presence of Atahualpa couriers to the four quarters of the Empire; and ere long, in answer, porters
began to appear bearing all manner of gold and silver objects: jars, vases, ewers, salvers, and goblets

from the temples; to say naught of hammered golden sheets, an occasional "throne," "pedestal," or "sun." They brought, too, wonderful things from the official dwellings — the "palaces" — of the Inca: such, for example, as "fountains designed to emit sparkling jets of gold"; miniature gold birds and beasts; trees also; plants with leaves, flowers, and fruit; fields of maize with leaves, heads, canes, roots, and flowers; and flowers of the field with petals, stems, and leaves. So gleaming indeed were the long files of porters under their golden packs, that as beheld afar they seemed veritable threads of gold caught from point to point across the landscape.

A circumstance which helped materially in collecting the treasure was that Hernando Pizarro and Hernando de Soto had conceived for Atahualpa a genuine liking. A suite of rooms was assigned him, and within these he maintained his customary state. Here he amused himself with his concubines; here with great animation and skill he played dice and chess, games learned from his conquerors; and here he received his vassals in audience — none of whom, however great, presumed to enter before him without first removing his sandals and placing a burden on his back.

The point to which Atahualpa had agreed to fill
Pizarro's chamber with gold was some nine feet
from the floor, and the floor dimensions were about
seventeen by twenty-two feet. As this space of
over three thousand cubic feet began to gradually
lessen under the heaps and piles of gold thrown
into it, did Francisco Pizarro reflect? Twenty
years before — first in Comogre's country, then
on the peak in Darien, and finally on the shores
of the Gulf of San Miguel — he, a dutiful lieutenant to Balboa, had heard intimations of Peru, of
Peru the golden somewhere to the south. Since
then Balboa had forfeited his head, and he alone
had found Peru. Had Columbus found it, or Behaim, or Alonso Pinzón, how each would have
wrestled with geography to prove that he had
found, if not Cathay and Cipangu, at least India,
at least the Golden Chersonese! Columbus on his
fourth voyage would have seen in Peru — capping
"the stem of the earth," as from its altitude it
might well have been thought to do — the "Earthly Paradise"; and to Cortés, had he found it,
it would have answered, more even than did
Mexico, to the requirements of that land whence
"Solomon is said to have brought the gold for
the Temple."

It took longer to fill Pizarro's chamber with gold up to the nine-foot point than Atahualpa had counted on, for, as the drain became severe, the public guardians, especially in the temples, began to secrete their treasures. At length, Pizarro waxing highly impatient, Atahualpa, who too was impatient, proposed that the former send out collectors of his own. They might go to Pachacamac, Peru's shrine to "an unknown god," very ancient and very rich; or they might go directly to Cuzco, where more than anywhere else the gold and silver of the Inca government was massed; and at either place they might help themselves. They went to both places, and what they brought back was, from Pachacamac, twenty-seven loads (*cargas*) of gold and two thousand marks of silver; and from Cuzco, two hundred loads of gold and twenty-five loads of silver. A "load" (333 pounds) was what could be carried by four Indians, and as part of several such loads from Cuzco there were brought seven hundred gold plates stripped from the Temple of the Sun, each plate being ten or twelve inches wide, and weighing from four to twelve pounds.

It was now June, 1533, and although the nine-foot level in Pizarro's chamber was not yet quite

attained, it was deemed expedient to melt down the
collection and value it preparatory to a division.
So valued, it reached a total of 1,326,539 *pesos de
oro;* or, counting the purchasing power of a peso as
$11.67, nearly $15,500,000 in American money.
Nor did this include the silver of the smaller chamber, which was estimated at 51,610 marks. No such
treasure had ever before been amassed by a conqueror. So gigantic was it, so staggering, that had
Pizarro sought for it a parallel, he must needs have
betaken himself, not to Marco Polo's East or that
of Ibn Batuta, but to the East of the Arabian
Nights Entertainments. "The genie [so runs a
familiar tale] returned with forty black slaves each
bearing on his head a heavy tray of pure gold; . . .
each tray was covered with silver tissue embroidered with flowers of gold. . . . The genie disappeared but presently returned with the forty
slaves, ten of whom carried each a purse containing a thousand pieces of gold. . . . But most of
all to be coveted were four large buffets profusely
furnished with large flagons, basins, and cups, all
of massy gold." So was it with Aladdin, and
so, without hyperbole, was it with Pizarro.

Desiring to impress his King with the wealth of
Peru, that Peru which he alone had conquered,

Pizarro, in the same year in which he melted down his treasure, sent to Spain his brother Hernando with the fifth portion belonging to the Crown and with half a million *pesos de oro* besides. The custom-house at Seville, it is said, overflowed with "solid ingots," not to mention "vases, animals, flowers, and fountains, all of pure gold." The populace were dazed; the Court aghast, for successful adventurers were not loved at Court; and the King, delighted. Cortés had created a flurry with his "wheels of gold and silver" sent home in 1519; and had all of his "gleanings" from Montezuma been got together in one place and at one time, they would have made an enduring impression. But for the most part Spain never saw them, for they were either captured by Francis I of France or lost during the *noche triste*. When Cortés and Pizarro met at Palos, in 1528, the cry in Spain was all "Cortés and Mexico!" After the coming of Hernando Pizarro to Seville, in 1534, the tables were completely turned. The cry then, and ever after as long as Cortés and Pizarro lived, was "Pizarro and Peru!"

But to go back a little. It was midsummer, 1533, and Pizarro had decided to march to Cuzco,

his real objective since the day when Bartolomé
Ruiz had heard of it and its splendor from the
Indians on the raft off Tumbez. Seven full months
had he lingered at Caxamarca, and all the gold
that could be gathered there he had obtained.
Besides, Almagro was again in Peru. He had
landed late in December, 1532, with three ships
piloted by Ruiz, and with a force consisting of
one hundred and fifty foot-soldiers and fifty horsemen. Pizarro was glad of the reënforcement.
Whether he was glad of the personal presence of
Almagro is not so certain. Almagro was Pizarro's
"partner" — his only active partner, for Luque
was now dead — and, to apply the motto of
the present chapter, "he that has partners has
masters."

If Almagro was Pizarro's "master," this was a
relationship for the future to disclose. Up to the
present Almagro's only recompense for toil and a
lost eye had been the captaincy of Tumbez, whatever that might import, and against Pizarro his
soul was bitter. Nor was the news which greeted
him at San Miguel, whither he came from Tumbez,
of a sort to appease. Pizarro had scaled the Andes;
had seized the Inca of Peru; and from the latter
was exacting an enormous ransom. In these

momentous transactions, where did Almagro, Pizarro's "partner," figure? Did he figure at all? Almagro determined to see. With his men he, too, scaled the Andes and in February, 1533, was at Caxamarca. Hence Pizarro's decision to march to Cuzco; for not only had he exhausted the gold to be obtained at Caxamarca, but, in order to meet the expectations and demands of his followers, now by Almagro's arrival quite doubled in number, he needed yet more gold. Of the fifteen and one-half million dollars in Pizarro's hands, as revealed by the melting down and weighing of his main treasure, Almagro's company would seem to have been quieted with some two hundred and thirty-three thousand dollars. Their harvest, it was explained to them, awaited them in Cuzco. What Almagro himself consented to receive is nowhere told. To Pizarro and his men, as those by whom thus far the conquest had actually been achieved, there fell immense sums: to Pizarro himself, nearly seven hundred thousand dollars, to say nothing of two thousand three hundred marks of silver; to Hernando Pizarro, nearly three hundred and sixty-three thousand dollars, without counting silver; to De Soto, two hundred and seventy thousand dollars, not counting silver; to each horseman, one hundred and three thousand dollars; and to the foot-soldiers, the most meritorious of them, nearly fifty-two thousand dollars each.

And now on every hand, and especially from Almagro's contingent, the cry arose: "On to Cuzco!" "But," said Pizarro, "wait! What about Atahualpa?"

The Indian monarch had in substance, if not in letter, kept his word regarding his ransom and was now demanding freedom. Should freedom be given him? Early in his captivity the news that he was paying vast sums to Pizarro as a ransom had come to the ears of the legitimate Inca, who was in captivity near Cuzco; and Huascar, proceeding to do what Atahualpa had surmised he might, had surreptitiously entered into relations with the Spaniards and offered a greater ransom for freedom than the ransom offered by Atahualpa. What a situation was here! And how completely to the Spanish advantage! It admitted the playing off of one hostile element against another, and a Spaniard like Cortés would have triumphed by it. But Pizarro was not Cortés. What he did was to leave Huascar in Atahualpa's power, and at the same time incautiously let it be known to Atahualpa that Huascar was outbidding him. The

natural result followed: Huascar, by order of Atahualpa, was quietly put to death.

Atahualpa at liberty must in any event be to the
Spaniards no small menace; but, with Huascar out
of the way, the menace was yet greater. What
should be done with him? The general voice was
for killing him. Against this some protested —
notably Hernando de Soto; and had Hernando
Pizarro been then in Peru, his protest probably
would have backed that of De Soto. But the
general voice so far prevailed that in August the
Inca was brought to trial. Some of the charges
against him were unfair, as for example that he
was an idolater and that he kept concubines; but
two of them may have been genuinely conceived:
one that he had injured the Spaniards by diverting
part of his treasure; and the other, that he had
done so by the murder of Huascar. A final charge
there was, and its genuineness was manifest, to
wit, that he was plotting an insurrection against
Spanish rule.

The result of the proceedings was that Atahualpa was found guilty and was condemned to
death at the stake. But on his recanting his own
faith and professing himself a Christian, his sen-
tence was commuted. At night, on August 29,

1533, in the plaza of Caxamarca, he was strangled with a bowstring.

For the march to Cuzco all at last was clear. A start was set for early in September, and when the day arrived loud did the Spanish bugles shout from their golden throats. No more uncertainty! No more delay! Ho now for El Dorado! Ho for regal Cuzco and the Temple of the Sun! The way along the Quito-Cuzco road was precipitous, and owing to the cliffs and stairways, chasms and raging torrents — the latter spanned only by swaying bridges of osier — the Spanish force of nearly five hundred men had much ado to keep a footing. Nor was this all. On the march the Conqueror was much harassed by Indian attacks, and, suspecting these to be instigated by one of Atahualpa's captains, Challcuchima by name, whom he had with him as a hostage, he ruthlessly destroyed that worthy by burning him at the stake.

Pizarro entered Cuzco two hours before sunset on November 15, 1533, a year to a day from the time when he had entered Caxamarca. How did this capital of the Incas look to him? Situated a hundred and fifty miles northwest of Titicaca, it lay in a valley dominated by steep hills and distant mountains. On one of the hills reposed a huge Cyclopean fortress, Sacsahuaman, accentuated by towers square and round, a relic of that Megalithic or Great Stone Age which preceded the Inca period. But what presumably attracted Pizarro most were the structures of the town itself, the palaces and temples wherein lay the treasure. Grouped in the main about a plaza, with heavy inward-sloping stone walls pierced by doorways broader at bottom than top, they made a picture that was curiously Egyptian. These buildings were numerous, too, for not only was the town large — over a hundred thousand souls, perhaps — but when any great Cuzcan died, Inca or nobleman, his abode passed to no successor but was maintained in all respects as though he were yet alive.

Far more than Mexico-Tenochtitlan was Cuzco a holy city. The supremacy there of one religious cult, Sun worship, fostered monotheism, and monotheism demanded a supreme temple. Hence that shrine of the Sun, noblest edifice in America since the days of splendor in Yucatán, a sight of which the Spaniards had so ardently craved. There now it lay in a court of flowers, one end rounded into an apse, its outer wall embellished by a golden cornice three feet in depth. Pizarro must soon have visited the interior — that interior whence largely had come the seven hundred golden plates, and where now was to be seen the Sun himself in the guise of a resplendent golden disc flanked by mummies of Incas, his departed children, posed on golden thrones, sustained by golden pedestals.

But in Cuzco religion did not exhaust itself with one temple, even though that temple was supreme. The whole city reflected religion — indeed was based upon it. So true was this, that the Center, the "Polaris" of the Empire, as distinguished from the "Four Quarters," was the center of the plaza of Cuzco. Here, in the form of a golden vase, was a fountain; and about this, before dawn on the day of the summer solstice, Peruvians were wont to gather by tribes to worship. And to worship what? Not an image of the Sun, but the Sun himself, if perchance he should appear. That he would appear was not taken for granted. He might not. Would he show his face on this great day? Anxiety reigned, dread even. Then "over the mountains the silent herald Dawn, and — following — the Sun!" All very splendid, but not anything that Pizarro saw or would have rejoiced in had he seen it. To him, no less than to Father Valverde, the whole ceremony would have been utter infidelity, rank idolatry, a celebration to be straightway suppressed, as in fact it was.

With regard to the treasure actually uncovered at Cuzco or on the way thither — slabs of silver twenty feet long by one foot broad, gold-enwrapped mummies of Inca queens, and other precious objects — the quantity was vast, but not so vast, not by half, as the quantity already divided. Almagro's men, by waiting for their harvest until Cuzco was reached, did not fare as well as they would have fared at Caxamarca. Certain it is, though, that they fared too well to show signs of discontent. Discontent on their part, when it came, as come it inevitably did, was from a cause quite different.

Three definite stages of the Peruvian conquest there were: that of preparation, that of active hostilities, and that of accomplishment. It is, however, a peculiarity of this conquest that the last stage, that of amassing treasure and of seizing dominion, instead of following upon the state of active hostilities, largely preceded it and gave rise to it. Now, therefore, for a glance at the stage of active hostilities. Here Pizarro does not shine as he did in the preparatory stage of patience and endurance. A new man dominates the scene, Pizarro's brother, Hernando.

Hernando Pizarro is ever a figure knightly and romantic. Unlike the rest of his family, he was neither illegitimate nor ignorant, though like them he was poor and had his way to make. That he could be chivalrous appears from his attitude toward Atahualpa, an attitude shared by an associate, Hernando do Soto. In these of our pages devoted to Mexico and Peru, three figures stand out as representatives of that chivalry illustrated in the *Amadis of Gaul* and satirized in *Don Quixote:* not so much Vasco Nuñez de Balboa, Hernan Cortés, and Francisco Pizarro as, rather, Juan de Grijalva, Hernando de Soto, and Hernando Pizarro, men whom we instinctively associate with scenes of the tourney, with "splintered spear-shafts," and "shivered brands," but hardly less with "perfume and flowers that lightly rain from ladies' hands."

Hernando Pizarro it was, to cite an incident romantic as well as practical, who, on the expedition which he led to Pachacamac, gave the memorable order that the Spanish horses were to be shod with silver in lieu of iron. Hernando Pizarro, too, it was who, as Pizarro's emissary to

Spain, performed with courtliness the duty of laying at the royal feet the incomparable riches of the Incas. A further duty in Spain he discharged, and one surely not lacking in chivalry: he assented to and even promoted the interests of Almagro, whom he did not like, by joining with the latter's agent in procuring for him, along with the title of Mariscal or Marshal, a grant of two hundred leagues beginning where Pizarro's grant left off. But where did Pizarro's grant leave off? To this question the answer involves much: the story of Peru to the death of Almagro; then to the imprisonment of Hernando Pizarro for that death; and finally to the death of the Conqueror himself.

Returning from Spain in the summer of 1535, Hernando Pizarro brought with him orders extending the jurisdiction of Pizarro seventy leagues beyond the two hundred to the south of the River Santiago earlier allotted him, and bestowing upon him the title of Marqués de los Atavillos. But already at Cuzco it had come to Almagro's knowledge, and hence to Pizarro's, that the former had received a grant to the south of that of Pizarro. Therefore the question: Did two hundred and seventy leagues south from the River Santiago fall short of Cuzco, and so deliver that prize to

Almagro; or beyond it, and so confirm it to Pizarro? Contending strenuously that Cuzco fell to him, Almagro nevertheless, soon after June, 1535, set out for Chile, a land possibly richer than Peru, one in any event undeniably his to exploit. De Soto, eager for adventure, would fain have gone with the Marshal but failed to gain consent. There did go, however, an auxiliary party of natives under the chief medicine-man of Cuzco, the Villac Umu.

Such, as between the partners Pizarro and Almagro, was the situation when Pizarro found himself beset by another difficulty. The Indians of Peru were at last awake. In behalf of their land and their religion, of the ashes of their fathers and the temples of their gods, they had begun against the Spaniards a mighty revolt.

By the time this revolt broke forth on April 18, 1536, Pizarro had accomplished three considerable undertakings, or rather one such undertaking, for the other two had been accomplished for him rather than by him. Late in 1533, or early in 1534, Sebastián de Benalcazar had seized Quito. Then Pedro de Alvarado, our earlier acquaintance, blond and daredevil, having heard of Quito as a rich quarry, had disembarked against it at

Caraques, but had been headed off by Almagro backed by Benalcazar, and for a consideration called "his expenses," had agreed to leave the country. Lastly, on January 6, 1535, Pizarro had founded as the capital of Peru the city of Lima.

But to seize the thread of our story. On the execution of Atahualpa, Pizarro found that while a captive Inca might be an embarrassment, no Inca at all would be a greater embarrassment still. He thereupon promptly filled the place of the dead Inca by naming as his successor one of Atahualpa's brothers, Toparca. On the way to Cuzco Toparca died, and a brother to the murdered Huascar — called Manco Inca — coming forth to greet Pizarro with professions of loyalty, was accepted as Inca and received the *borla*. Manco Inca, with studied Indian craft, disarmed Spanish caution and laid deep and secret plans.

In 1536 Hernando Pizarro commanded in Cuzco, where were also his brothers, Juan and Gonzalo; and, though by this time Manco Inca had in a measure betrayed his hand, Hernando in his chivalrous way treated him with confidence. On the 18th of April, Manco, in company with his chief medicine-man, who had left Almagro, quietly departed from Cuzco, on a pretext of visiting the

burial-place of Huayna Ccapac, and once beyond
Pizarro's reach summoned in council the caciques
and war captains of Peru. "I am resolved,"
declared the Inca, "to rid this land of every Christian, and shall first lay siege to Cuzco." Then,
ordering to be brought two large golden vessels full
of wine, "let such as are with me," he exclaimed,
"pledge themselves herein to the death!"

The fight for Cuzco centered around the huge
fortress of Sacsahuaman. This, at first, the Indians were able to seize and hold by setting on fire
the combustible thatched roofs of the town and so
forcing the Spaniards to huddle together in the
plaza. But after a week of mingled struggle and
endurance the fortress was scaled and captured.
Its last defender was a Peruvian of giant size and
prowess, one of the war chiefs who had pledged
himself in the wine. This hero, seeing all was lost,
"sprinkled dust upon his head toward heaven,"
then cast himself down upon the foe and so
perished.

While Hernando Pizarro was defending Cuzco,
his brother the Conqueror was at Lima, his new
capital. Here he was besieged; but the country
being level, he was able to beat off the enemies by
the aid of his horsemen. His great concern was

Cuzco. Thither he dispatched what aid he could, but with ill success, for the party was intercepted and the severed heads of divers of them were thrown at Hernando's feet. But he did more. He appealed for aid to the entire world of Spanish America — to Panamá, to Nicaragua, to Guatemala, to New Spain, and to Española. That is to say, he appealed among others to Pedro de Alvarado and to Hernan Cortés; and by Cortés at least aid was sent.

In the struggle for Cuzco, Indian warfare was exhibited to Europeans on a scale hitherto unparalleled. Not alone were there warriors in countless masses. Such had there been in Mexico. Not alone were there tossing crests, waving banners, and panoplies of featherwork. Such had there been in Mexico. Not alone were there forests of long lances and battle-axes edged with copper. Such things, or similar, had there been in Mexico. But there was displayed something besides — something which in Mexico had not been quite the same — to wit, real military intelligence. Though in general softer of fiber than the Aztec, both intellectually and physically, the Peruvian sometimes outdid the Aztec in wit. To the Peruvian, for example, the "white stranger" was less a preternatural being than to the Aztec. The former, too, feared the horse somewhat less. It is even said by Herrera that, so accustomed to the horse had the Peruvian become by the time of the struggle for Cuzco that he was occasionally to be seen on horseback himself, a statement which Sir Arthur Helps distinctly challenges.

But the circumstances most significant for us in the Cuzco battles — battles hotly contested, for in one of them Juan Pizarro was killed — are the skill, the valor, the caution, the perseverance, and the knightly bearing of Hernando Pizarro. This capable leadership, especially in its knightly aspect, appears to an even higher degree, however, in the contest next to arise, one in which the Peruvian forces were divided between warring factions of the invading Spaniards.

It was 1537, and Almagro was back from Chile. Weary, starved, frost-bitten, sun-blistered, disillusioned, and disgusted, he had returned. No more chasing of will-o'-the-wisps for him! Cuzco fell within his province! He knew it, so Cuzco he would have! Seeking but failing to make friends with Manco Inca, who lay with a strong force outside the city, Almagro overthrew him in fight, and, disregarding an armistice with Hernando Pizarro for an adjustment of boundaries by "pilots," on the stormy night of the 8th of April he stole into Cuzco and, surprising Hernando and Gonzalo Pizarro in their beds, promptly seized them and imprisoned them in the Temple of the Sun.

The feud long maturing between the partners Pizarro and Almagro was now squarely at issue. First, Almagro defeated Pizarro's lieutenant, Alonso de Alvarado, and thereby made his tenancy of Cuzco secure. Next, Gaspar de Espinosa, Luque's successor in the partnership, arriving from Panamá, sought to reconcile Almagro with Pizarro, but died in the midst of his efforts. Then Almagro, becoming aware of Pizarro's increasing force, consented to arbitration. Over this the partners met, embraced one another, and wept. There had in the past been many meetings of reconciliation between Pizarro and Almagro, and at all of them tears had been freely shed. Once the partners had even had recourse to the Church, and had divided between them the Host. Nor were these meetings all mere fustian and hypocrisy. Not at any rate with Almagro. Old, ugly, scarred, and of inferior physique, he was at the same time capable of feeling and of manifesting the profoundest generosity.

Despite tears and embraces, the arbitration had not succeeded; but a treaty was made whereby Hernando and Gonzalo Pizarro were set at liberty on stipulation that the question of Cuzco be left to the King and that Hernando Pizarro leave Peru within six weeks. Then suddenly there developed a further phase in the Pizarro-Almagro feud. Hardly had the treaty been concluded when a messenger from Spain brought word that each partner was to retain what he had already conquered and peopled. Both hereupon claimed to have conquered Cuzco; and Pizarro, having the stronger following, declared the treaty annulled and prepared for battle.

The principal commanders on the side of Pizarro, who had himself withdrawn to Lima on account of his years, were Hernando and Gonzalo Pizarro, Alonso de Alvarado, and Pedro de Valdivia. On the side of Almagro, they were Almagro himself, too much incapacitated to fight but watching the field from afar in a litter; Pedro de Lerma, a deserter from Pizarro; and above all Rodrigo de Orgañez, a doughty, implacable soldier trained under the Constable of Bourbon. As for the forces, they were nearly equal: on Pizarro's side, some six hundred and fifty men; and on Almagro's, six hundred and eighty; whereof about two hundred and eighty and three hundred, respectively, were horsemen.

Battle was joined on April 6, 1538, a short way out of Cuzco on the Plains of Salinas, and by the encounter that took place such cavaliers as Hernando Pizarro, Rodrigo de Orgañez, and Pedro de Lerma must have been reminded of combats in the Old World. One circumstance, however, rendered it peculiarly a New World combat. Almagro's men, divers of them, wore corslets, morions, and arm-pieces hammered out of silver. By doubling the quantity of silver used, as compared with iron, they succeeded in producing, so they said, an armor as strong as that forged at Milan. In any event, it was as pretty a *mêlée* of knights, gentlemen, and foot-soldiers as one might wish to see; for not only were there skill and prowess, but, as occurs not seldom in partnership readjustments, a becoming amount of deadly animosity.

But, more particularly, what of Hernando Pizarro? "A veray parfit gentil knight" Hernando was and, as such, careful of his appearance. Over his corslet he wore a surcoat of orange damask. Fastened to this was the Cross of the Order of Santiago given him by the King; and above his morion floated a tall white plume. These embellishments looked well, but there was more to them than that. Being a true Sir Knight, he had wrongs to avenge, and he wished his enemies to be able to distinguish him easily in the press and to have every opportunity to encounter him. At one point only was he at a disadvantage and a bit of a Don Quixote. He was not handsome. He was tall, which was well; but his lips hung heavy, and his nose was bulbous and red at the end.

The challenge of the flame-colored surcoat and white plume did not pass unheeded. Pedro de Lerma spurred against Pizarro, with whom his relations were peculiarly strained, and Pizarro spurred against Lerma. The lance of Lerma took effect chiefly upon Pizarro's horse, forcing him back on his haunches and unseating the rider, while Pizarro's lance pierced his adversary's thigh. Indeed this special bout was a kind of Ivanhoe and Brian de Bois-Guilbert affair, for neither combatant quite overcame the other; and the unhorsed knight, springing erect, drew his sword to try conclusions on foot.

Organez meanwhile, grim and sinister, was

14

himself seeking Pizarro. His training had been in a harsh school which believed that "dead men do not bite," and when Hernando was in Almagro's power, Orgañez had urgently advised cutting off his head. Like Richard of Gloucester at Bosworth Field, Orgañez at Salinas would seem to have been haunted by a presentiment that he was doomed to die. First, though, he would kill the usurper Pizarro. His rushes therefore were headlong and fierce. One cavalier whom, from a bright surcoat, he thought to be Hernando, he charged and ran through. Another he likewise pierced with his lance; and a third he cut down with his sword. Then, wounded in the head by a chain-shot, and his horse being down, he yielded to numbers. His sword he delivered up to one of Pizarro's squires, a cowardly fellow who stabbed his helpless prisoner to the heart.

Throughout the battle, the hills about the Plains of Salinas were covered by onlooking Indians, auxiliaries of Almagro; but they merely looked on and wondered and took no part. The more the Spaniards slaughtered one another, the greater the gain to the natives. And, considering the numbers engaged, the slaughter was great. In less than two hours, more than one hundred and fifty knights

and foot-soldiers were killed outright. Lerma
received seventeen wounds and escaped, only to be
murdered in his bed after the battle. Then came
Almagro's turn — not that he was immediately
made way with, but was put in prison and treated
with consideration. In connection with his imprisonment severe criticism has been visited upon
Hernando Pizarro. In Cuzco there were many
Almagrists, and, so long as their leader lived, peril
to the stability of the Pizarro régime was imminent.
Plots for the prisoner's liberation were rife. Under
these circumstances Hernando Pizarro, disregarding tears, pleas for mercy, and reminders of how
his own life had been spared by Almagro, permitted
the latter to be condemned to death. Whether in
so doing Hernando was actuated by a sense of
duty or was simply displaying something of Spanish primitivism, a quality so conspicuous in Pedrarias, is a question. On July 8, 1538, Diego de
Almagro was strangled in prison, and the next day
the body was shown in the plaza with the head
cut off.

Almagro, dead, was now more his partner's
"master" than he had been when alive. Hernando
Pizarro sailed in 1539 for Spain to explain matters

to the King. He was, however, anticipated by a friend of the dead partner, Diego de Alvarado, and was coldly received. Alvarado on his part challenged Hernando to mortal combat but died before the ordeal of battle could be essayed. Yet Hernando Pizarro did not escape punishment for the death of Almagro but was shut up in the fortress of Medina del Campo, where he was kept a prisoner for twenty years.

On leaving Peru, Hernando Pizarro had cautioned his brother the Conqueror, to "beware the men of Chile," the Almagrists. They formed a distinct element both in Cuzco and in Lima, and at the latter place under the leadership of Juan de Rada, the one-time follower of Cortés, dreamed and conspired against the Conqueror's life. Finally, on June 26, 1541, their plottings bore fruit. On that day at noon, to the number of eighteen or twenty, they surprised Pizarro in the government house and slew him in cold blood. With the Conqueror at the time were several persons, notably his brother Martín of Alcantara, the least prominent of the family, but like all of them valiant and a good swordsman. The onset of the conspirators was furious. Pizarro was not able so much as to secure the door against them or to put on his

corslet. Martín fought desperately but was soon
cut down. Thereupon Pizarro, wrapping his left
arm in his cloak, seized his sword and did bloody
execution; but at length, receiving a thrust in the
neck, he fell to the floor. "Jesu!" exclaimed the
fallen Conqueror, and, tracing on the floor a cross
in his own blood, he bent to kiss it and so died.

Of the four brothers of Pizarro, two were now
dead and one was in permanent confinement in
Spain. There was left in Peru Gonzalo Pizarro
only. His career, like that of the Conqueror, was
chequered. In 1540, in obedience to orders, he had
made exploration from the Andes eastward. On
this expedition one of his lieutenants, Francisco de
Orellana, sailed down a stream traversing a country where "the women fought by the side of their
husbands," a country of Amazons, and at length
passed into the Atlantic Ocean. In 1544 Gonzalo
Pizarro made himself Governor of Peru. He as-
pired, it is said, to become its absolute ruler and
lord; and had he but heeded the counsel of his
master of the camp, Francisco de Carvajal, he
might have succeeded. As it was, in April, 1548,
he was defeated in battle by forces of the Crown
and was beheaded. The same year in which

Gonzalo Pizarro had gone eastward from Quito, another explorer, Pedro de Valdivia, had gone southward into Chile; and here, on September 3, 1544, he founded the city of Valparaíso. In 1547 Valdivia returned to Peru and was instrumental in bringing defeat on Gonzalo Pizarro.

With regard to the Almagrist party, on the execution of their leader, they set up his natural son Diego as Governor, but he was pronounced a rebel by the Crown, and in 1542, after the death of his able supporter, Juan de Rada, was overthrown in battle, captured, and put to death. In this conflict our old acquaintance Pedro de Candia was Almagro's artillerist, but, falling under suspicion of treachery, was ridden down and killed by Almagro himself.

From among the interesting figures in Peru under the Pizarro régime, there remains to be accounted for only the Inca Manco. Not long after his defeat by Almagro, he took refuge in a fastness of the Andes. The spot, it is thought, was the Megalithic town of Machu Picchu, whence the Incas had sprung. Here with his concubines, the Virgins of the Sun, he kept court, receiving and succoring outlawed Spaniards, beings no longer regarded by any Indian as preternatural. Here, too, about 1544, he died — struck down, it is said, at a game of bowls by a Spaniard with whom he had an altercation.

After 1545, zeal for conquest in America on the part of Spain tended perceptibly to die down. As early as 1535, well within the lifetime of Cortés, who did not die till 1547, a Viceroy had been sent to Mexico. One was sent to Peru in 1543. With these appointments, government in Spanish-America gradually became more stable. Vast now, seemingly, was the interval since the day when, responding to the lure of Antillia, of Cipangu, and of the Cathay of Março Polo, Columbus had set sail from Palos for

The land where the sunsets go.

BIBLIOGRAPHICAL NOTE

OF the region of the West — the Atlantic Ocean or Sea of Darkness — John Fiske, *The Discovery of America*, 2 vols. (1899), presents a fascinating account; and cartographical points are considered in great detail by Justin Winsor, *Narrative and Critical History of America*, 8 vols. (1884–1889), vols. I and II, and *Christopher Columbus* (1891). The subject of Mythical Islands in the Atlantic, a subject of growing importance, is interestingly treated by Sir Clements R. Markham, *Life of Christopher Columbus* (1892), but its bearing on the discovery of America is best brought out in two magazine articles of recent date: one by William H. Babcock (*Scottish Geographical Magazine*, vols. XXXI and XXXII, 1915–1916), and the other by Thomas J. Westropp, *Brazil and the Legendary Isles of North America* (*Proceedings of the Royal Irish Academy*, 1912).

The above-cited discussions are apart from the question of the Northmen in America, for, while the Northmen no doubt discovered parts of North America at a very early date, these discoveries had no bearing on the discovery by Columbus. The pre-Columbian discoveries (or discoveries by the Northmen) may be found well set forth by Julius E. Olson, *The Northmen, Columbus, and Cabot* (*Original Narratives of Early American History*, 1906), where authorities are given.

As regards the East — Asia and India before Columbus — Sir Henry Yule, *The Book of Ser Marco Polo*, 2 vols. (3d ed. revised by Henri Cordier, 1903), and Yule, *Cathay and the Way Thither*, 4 vols. (revised by Cordier, *Hakluyt Society Pubs.*, 1916), and R. H. Major, vol. XXII, *India in the Fifteenth Century* (*Hakluyt Soc. Pubs.*, 1857) are fundamental. The same subject is more briefly treated by Cheyney, *The European Background of American History* (1904), and by John Fiske, *The Discovery of America*. Voyages to the East by the Portuguese are entertainingly described by R. H. Major, *Life of Prince Henry of Portugal* (1868).

COLUMBUS

Authoritative lives of Columbus in English are few. The best known is by Washington Irving, *Life and Voyages of Christopher Columbus*, 2 vols. (1828–1831). Based on original sources, this charming narrative, once authoritative, is now to a great degree superseded. The best life for the modern general reader is probably that by Sir Clements R. Markham, *Life of Christopher Columbus* (1892). John Fiske, *The Discovery of America*, presents a highly sympathetic portrait of Columbus. Beginning with 1884 lives of Columbus have been less sympathetic in form and more critical. In that year Henry Harrisse published *Christophe Colomb*, 2 vols. This has not been translated, but in 1892 was followed by his *Discovery of North America*, in three parts, a work in English. Following this appeared in English a still more critical estimate of Columbus by Henry Vignaud, *Toscanelli and Columbus* (1902). Then came Vignaud's *Études critiques sur la vie de Colomb* (1905) and *Histoire critique de la grande entreprise de Christophe Colomb*, 2 vols. (1911). The views of Mr. Harrisse are strongly reflected by Justin Winsor, *Christopher Columbus* (1892). Influenced by the views of Mr. Harrisse and of Mr. Vignaud, Filson Young published in 1906 *Christopher Columbus and the New World of his Discovery*, 2 vols. (3d ed., 1912), a narrative written in popular style. To this is appended a valuable note by the Earl of Dunraven on the seamanship of Columbus's first voyage.

But there have not been wanting writers to combat the iconoclasm of the critical lives of Columbus, as for example: John Boyd Thacher, *Christopher Columbus*, 3 vols. (1903–1904); Henry P. Biggar, *The New Columbus* (*Report of the American Historical Association*, 1912). Valuable critical estimates of the opinions of Vignaud and Thacher may be found expressed by Edward Gaylord Bourne in the *American Historical Review*, vol. VIII, 1903; vol. IX, 1904; vol. X, 1904; and in his *Spain in America* (*The American Nation Series*, 1904). Mr. Vignaud himself (*American Historical Review*, vol. XVIII, 1913) discusses claims made in certain quarters that Columbus was a Jew and in other quarters that he was a Spaniard. A vivid presentation of Columbus from an Italian source is contained in an article by Cesare de Lollis in the French *Revue des Revues*, January 15, 1898.

As bearing upon the early years of the life of Columbus, there is a valuable essay by Ravenstein, *Martin Behaim, his Life and his Globe* (1908). This work is especially noteworthy for a beautiful and accurate reproduction in colors of the gores of Behaim's globe, showing geographical conditions as conceived by Behaim in 1492, prior to Columbus's first voyage.

Source materials for the life of Columbus are extensive, but are largely in foreign tongues. *The Life of Columbus*, by Ferdinand Columbus, his son, may be found in English in Churchill, *Voyages* (1744–1746) and in Pinkerton, *Voyages* (1808–1814). Thacher's *Christopher Columbus* contains excellent translations of much early material, such as the earliest sketches of the life of Columbus by contemporaries: Las Casas's account of the discovery of America and of Columbus's third voyage; and excerpts from the *Epistles of Peter Martyr* on the discovery. Peter Martyr's *Decades*, translated by Richard Eden, 1555, and Michael Lok — highly entertaining — is accessible in Hakluyt, *Voyages* (vol. v, edition of 1812), and in *De Orbe Novo*, well translated by Francis Augustus MacNutt, 2 vols. (1912). Columbus's own letters, several of the most important, are printed in English by R. H. Major, *Select Letters of Columbus* (2d ed., 1890). Columbus's journal of his first voyage was printed in English by Sir Clements R. Markham, *Journal of Columbus* (1893); but a new and more literal translation is furnished by Thacher in his life of Columbus. By far the best account in English of Columbus's four voyages is that in the collection of documents edited by E. G. Bourne and printed in *The Northmen, Columbus, and Cabot* (*Original Narratives of Early American History*, 1906). In 1894 the American Historical Association printed in translation a number of the private letters of Columbus in its Annual Report.

BALBOA AND THE PACIFIC

For the voyages secondary to those of Columbus, the best authorities are the following: Irving, *Voyages of the Companions of Columbus* (1831), printed with Irving's *Life of Columbus;* Sir Arthur Helps, *The Spanish Conquest in America* (4 vols., 1855–1861, new edition with notes by M. Oppenheim, 4 vols., 1904), and H. H. Bancroft, *History of Central America*, 2 vols. (1882–1887). The voyages of Ojeda and Nicuesa, involving Balboa, are covered by the authorities just cited. Peter Martyr's *Decades* contains an admirable sketch of Balboa and his discovery of the Pacific Ocean. The latest and most authoritative account (especially as to chronology) is, however, in Spanish by the Chilean scholar, J. T. Medina, *El Descubrimiento del Océano Pacifico*.

NAMING OF AMERICA

Vespucci and the naming of America has given rise to much discussion. John Fiske, following the Brazilian scholar Varnhagen, treats the subject controversially in *The Discovery of America*. His views are critically reviewed by E. G. Bourne in his *Spain in America*. The latest treatment (one favorable to Vespucci) is by Vignaud, *Améric Vespuce (1451–1512)* (1917), a work in French. It is Mr. Vignaud's thesis that not only did Vespucci anticipate Columbus in the discovery of the mainland of America, but that he, first of all explorers and writers, realized that Mundus Novus (South America) was wholly distinct from Asia, a new continent and a new world. The letters of Vespucci have been printed in English by C. R. Markham, *Letters of*

Peru

Peru on the historical side has not been neglected by investigators. The conquest is described by Pizarro's two secretaries and by Hernando Pizarro: *Reports on the Discovery of Peru*, translated and edited by Sir Clements R. Markham (*Hakluyt Soc. Pubs.*, 1872). The report by Secretary Pedro Sancho has lately been retranslated by Philip Ainsworth Means and published by the Cortés Society, 1917. A readable account is by Sir C. R. Markham (Winsor, *Narrative and Critical History of America*, vol. II). The story of the Incas themselves is told by Markham, *The Incas of Peru* (1910). John Fiske contrasts the Peruvian and Aztec civilizations in *The Discovery of America;* and Peruvian chronology is studied by P. A. Means, *Culture Sequence in the Andean Area* (*Proceedings of the Nineteenth Congress of Americanists*, 1917). This article is followed, in the same publication, by an excellent general survey of Inca Culture by Hiram Bingham of Yale University. W. H. Prescott, *A History of the Conquest of Peru*, 2 vols. (1847), is still a good work; and Sir Arthur Helps, *The Spanish Conquest in America*, is excellent in its account of Peru. It departs from Prescott in the view presented of Hernando Pizarro.

General

For additional titles, see the bibliographical references appended to the articles on *Central America, Mexico, Peru*, and *South America*, as well as those on *Balboa, Cortés, Columbus*, and *Magellan*, in *The Encyclopædia Britannica*, 11th Edition.

INDEX

15   225